C000172676

BUSBY'S LAST CRUSADE

FROM MUNICH TO WEMBLEY: A PICTORIAL HISTORY

JEFF CONNOR

ARENA SPORT

This edition first published in Great Britain in 2020 by
ARENA SPORT
An imprint of Birlinn Limited
West Newington House
10 Newington Road
Edinburgh
EH9 1QS
www.arenasportbooks.co.uk

ISBN: 9781909715899
eBook ISBN: 9781788853132

British Library Cataloguing-in-Publication Data
A catalogue record for this book is available on request from the British Library.

Designed and typeset by Terry Watson
www.palmerwatson.com

Cover and chapter typography: Flama by Mario Feliciano
www.felicianotype.com

Printed in Latvia by PNB Print Ltd

ACKNOWLEDGEMENTS

Sincere thanks go to Pete Burns of Arena Sport for help and suggestions with the content and Natalie Jones of Mirrorpix for her patience and supply of the images. Thanks, too, to my agent, Mark Stanton from The North.

IN THE BE

Munich means different things to different people. For my mother, who is 96 as I write this, it means Chamberlain, Hitler and 1938. For journalists I worked with at the Orlando Sentinel in Florida during the mid-80s it meant the Olympics of 1972 and a massacre (though some preferred to remember Mark Spitz and his five gold medals). The only Chamberlain Floridians seem to have heard of was the Wilt of basketball fame.

But if you ask a football fan, of any age and from any era, Munich means only one thing. It doesn't take long to become involved in the history and if anyone wishes to see the depths of that involvement try a visit to Old Trafford any 6 February. If there were no 'official' ceremony organised by Manchester United plc – in fact were there no plc at all – the faithful would still be there on that day.

There are all types. I met a young couple from Singapore who had been trailing a suitcase on wheels down Warwick Road and had asked for directions. There were middle-aged men who had taken time off work, pensioners and children of every age.

The ritual is always mirrored elsewhere: at Marakana stadium in Belgrade; on a cold day in Dudley, in Salford, Doncaster and Barnsley; by Liam Whelan's grave in Dublin's Glasnevin Cemetery and in Munich, close by the site of the tragedy at the village of Trudering. Irene Beevers, the sister of David Pegg, told me that when she visited her brother at Doncaster's Adwick-le-Street cemetery she would often find a single, fresh, red rose in the perforated holder on top of the grave. Irene knew why, but never managed to find out who.

Much of this has been chronicled so many times newspapers have struggled to find

GINNING

anything new about Munich. Not that that will stop them from trying, with or without the facts. On 6 February 2008, the *Daily Mail* spread two of its feature pages which included a photograph of 'the Busby Babes boarding the flight to Munich from which many of them would never return'. The image was indeed of Manchester United players boarding a plane to Munich . . . but was taken in 1959. They were heading for a fixture against Bayern Munich, their first match abroad since the disaster. Busby is there, along with assistant manager Jimmy Murphy and trainer Jack Crompton, who were not on the Munich flight of 1958. The *Daily Express* covered the anniversary with an image of a youthful Albert Scanlon 'who died after the plane crashed'. This was undoubtedly news to Scanlon who not only survived but was still alive 50 years later.

The Sun, inevitably, weighed in with a piece from an eye witness 'exonerating' Captain Thain after he had been blamed by the German authorities for not de-icing the aircraft's wings. In fact, the pilot had been cleared in 1968 and the quotes – from the German rescuer eye witness – had been lifted from Stanley Stewart's excellent 1986 book, *Air Disasters*.

How long will this go on? Forever, I would guess.

A photographer friend sent me an email on the day after United's home win against Huddersfield on 3 February 2018. He had attached a file showing images he had taken pre-match of notables gathering for the memorial ceremony: Harry Gregg, Bobby Charlton, Alex Ferguson, and Jose Mourinho along with directors (though not the owners), current players and fans. Using the sort of pun endemic to newspapers he had added a one-line caption: LAST OF THE TWO?

He obviously meant Gregg and Charlton, who were both in their 80s at the time. Gregg had later promised that this, the 60th anniversary, would be his last and so it proved. On 16 February 2020, the Last of the Two became Last of the One.

On the day Gregg died, I checked who was left: Charlton obviously, Vesna Lukic, the baby Gregg rescued from the blazing cabin, her mother Vera and, given that Vera was four-months pregnant at the time, a son, Zoran should be included. They all live in Serbia, part of the old Yugoslavia, and the last member of the cabin crew, air stewardess Rosemary Cheverton, is 86 and has lived in North Carolina for several years. Goalkeeper Ray Wood died in 2002, Albert Scanlon, the winger turned dock labourer, in 2009, Bill Foulkes, the coal miner turned defender, four years later. Frank Taylor, the only journalist to survive, died the same year as Wood.

Then the close family members, wives or girlfriends, along with the affiliates: Roger Byrne Jnr, son of the club's revered captain from cancer in 2011 and Sandy Busby, son of Sir Matt, from a heart attack in 2014. John Doherty, a Busby Babe from 1952 to '57 and a driving force behind fundraising efforts for survivors' and victims' families died in 2007. Munich memorial services were becoming like the Cenotaph on Armistice Day: lots of ceremony, but no survivors. Any journalist intent on writing a Munich piece today may struggle for quotes, but there are always the 'heroes' by proxy, people who insist they would have been on the flight but missed it for various reasons. In his autobiography, *Harry's Game*, Gregg railed at a former team-mate, 'an after-dinner speaker who has lived on it for years, claiming he would have gone to Yugoslavia but for injury'. Gregg wouldn't name the player in print, but Wilf McGuinness, one of the original Babes and later the manager, used to be popular at corporate hospitality functions where he would tell tales of his days at Old Trafford. He had often claimed he was listed to go to Belgrade and,

by implication, death. He was still making the same claims in 2019 during an interview with *The Guardian*'s Donald McRae (who should really have known better).

The former Old Trafford CEO, Martin Edwards, went one better. Talking to the *Mail on Sunday* in 2018 in an effort to plug his autobiography, he was asked about the 'grief of the Munich air disaster'. He obliged with this eye-raiser: his father, Louis, a family friend of Busby, 'might have been on the plane' had not a club director blocked his proposal to join the board. Do we thank that club director . . . or blame him? Louis was voted on to a grief-stricken board the day after the disaster and both father and son made millions out of the club. At varying times, too, Manchester police were, as they like to say, 'investigating allegations' against both men.

They were always willing to bend a knee to the history of Munich . . . but only when it suited them. Reading the *Mail on Sunday* piece, I remembered an enlightening inter-view with John Doherty in 2005 and in particular his description of his visit, eight years previously, to see Edwards at his home in Wilmslow. Doherty had been part of a con-sortium trying to find the means to support survivors and bereaved families financially. They hadn't been having much luck.

'I wanted to ask Martin Edwards about the likelihood of some sort of benefit game for them,' Doherty said. 'He replied: "But why now, John; why now, after all this time?"

'And I said: "Because they are fucking skint, that's why."'

Rosemary Cheverton, front right, with the three other surviving members of the BEA crew: Captain James Thain (left), Radio Officer Bill Rodgers and Stewardess Margaret Bellis (left). Cabin Steward Tom Cable was killed instantly and co-pilot Ken Rayment died in hospital five weeks later.

THE THREE M

USKETEERS

There were new players, new rivals and even new management, but some things never changed in Manchester: come match time David Meek of the *Manchester Evening News* would be following United and Peter Gardner, also of the *MEN*, would be covering City.

Meek, who was 88 when he died in 2018, did this for close to 40 years; Gardner, the whipper-snapper, managed a mere 28 and is still alive as I write this. They were good operators, as they say in the business and better known in the city than several current players.

Running reports (runners) on matchdays, particularly Saturdays, were amazing affairs: an open phone line from wherever United or City were playing, a copytaker at the other end taking down the report and, usually, a choice of three intros (win, lose or draw) ten minutes before the end. It was out on the streets 15 minutes later.

Monday to Friday involved follow-ups: communiques from the manager and his views on the match, injury checks, team news and interviews with players of choice (in the 60s, like the 50s, this was never refused). These sounded like the dream jobs in journalism . . . but there were limitations. Meek and Gardner travelled in the same team coach from match to match and were on friendly terms with players and management and this is never ideal. They could see and hear a lot, but would never dare use it. The first time Meek overstepped the mark and broke an 'exclusive' the club wanted to suppress, Busby immediately banned him from the team bus for life. Gardner had similar problems when Howard Kendall took over at Maine Road in 1989. On daily newspapers, too, the same football writers were often embedded to the same teams and it was never wise

◄ PREVIOUS PAGE
The public got sight of the statue for the first time three years after George Best's death in 2005 and 40 years after the European Cup win. 'That's as close as you'll get those three embracing each other,' said one wag to me, pointing at the statue and implying that Best, Law and Charlton were never the best of pals (though Law was friendly with just about anyone). The 'Holy Trinity', as some were brave enough to call it, was built by the Scottish sculptor Philip Jackson, who created a similar tribute to Sir Matt Busby.

to step out of line: the club management could make life difficult for you and instead of covering United or City you could end up at a Bury or a Bolton. This was one reason why George Best stories in the 70s were handled not by the Meeks and Gardners of the world but by news reporters for whom being banned by a football club meant absolutely nothing.

In George's case, news desks had soon realised that at some part of the week, whether on or off the field, there will be a Best story and they had better not miss it. The media's view of him was summed up by skysports.com after George died in 2005 and they were trying to flog a video of him: 'A close look at Northern Ireland and Manchester United genius George Best, who was as well known for his exploits off the field as he was on it.' His on-the-field exploits were certainly well known to me because I saw most of them. I

They got close enough in 2000 when all three were presented with lifetime achievement awards as part of the National Football Awards. The ceremony took place at half-time during the Premiership match against Newcastle United at Old Trafford. Goals from Ronny Johnsen and Andy Cole ensured a 2–0 win.

Kick-off time for the Big Three ahead of the 2–2 draw against Fulham at Craven Cottage on 27 March 1967. The smudger (a word he is said to have invented) on the left is legendary *Mirror* man Monte Fresco.

never came across him off the field and (unlike skysports. com) didn't feel qualified to discuss his exploits there. Most of that information was supplied by the tabloid press, a group resistant to accuracy. The broadsheets were no better. I can remember one piece in *The Guardian* in 2001 which shows the extent of the background newspapers were willing to go to. It was just after he 'had fallen off the wagon again' as they liked to put it in headmasterly tones: 'He participated in one heavy drinking session last Monday and continued consuming large amounts of alcohol throughout the week. He was seen drinking in pubs in Ballyhalbert and Donaghadee, near his home on the Ards peninsula, near Belfast.' Some of the reportage was bizarre.

Two packs a day celebrities like Kenneth Tynan or John Huston were never criticised for heavy smoking despite knowing that their emphysema (an illness) would kill them but Best was reviled for the alcoholism (a disease) that would kill him. Incidentally, if Best's infamous TV interview with Terry Wogan in 1990 proved anything it was that George wasn't much of a drinker.

George Best the teenager in 1964.

So how should we remember him now: the exploits on the field or those off it? The missed training sessions, the failed marriages, the arrests, the very public suicide . . . or the boy in a Northern Ireland shirt reducing Scotland to impotence in a European Championship qualifier and 'the slim, boyish, dark hair shining in the floodlights as he scythed through the Benfica defence' (David Meek)? Maybe we should remember George as we remember others whose real addiction was a dislike for convention: Charlie Parker or Louise Brooks or even Errol Flynn – beautiful and gifted but fatally flawed and whose true worth came only after death.

● Like every other unmarried man at Old Trafford during the Busby era Best was expected to live in digs. Number 9, Aycliffe Avenue, was a red-brick terrace in Chorlton-cum-Hardy, the home of Mrs Fullaway, her son Steven, George and his United team-mate David Sadler (who escaped by marrying local girl Christine Halliday in 1968). George had two spells at No.9, the second being early in 1971 after a series of misdemeanours.

He had deliberately missed a Division One match against Chelsea in January that year, gone into hiding and was eventually tracked down to the Islington flat of Sinéad Cusack, a member of the well-known Irish film, stage and television family.

When the United management did get George back to full-time work and the sanctimonious howling in the media had died down his penance was that he had to move back into digs.

Living with Mrs Fullaway, by all accounts, was a safer option than living with Sinéad Cusack.

A Best-less United, incidentally, won 2–1 at Chelsea.

Best used to joke that of all his action pictures Chelsea's Ron 'Chopper' Harris was in most of them. There was one particular goal against Chelsea at Old Trafford when Harris had been told (by Chelsea manager Tommy Docherty) that he was to follow Best everywhere. By half-time he was dizzy and then Harris to his credit later recalled: 'It was a cup game. He was running through on goal but he's slightly overrun the ball. I thought, "F****** hell, here's your chance, finally." So I've slid in and kicked him, waist high. But he's somehow ridden it, danced around Peter Bonetti and put it in. It was the opening clip on Grandstand for years — watching that, I was sure I'd catch him one day!'

This was the night George Best stole the global stage. It was 9 March 1966 and the European Cup quarter-final second leg at Estadio da Luz, Lisbon. United were 3–2 ahead on aggregate against a Benfica side that included the legendary Eusébio, and manager Matt Busby had ordered 'to keep it tight' early on. Best took no notice, scoring twice in the first 15 minutes (this was his second) with the others coming from John Connelly, Pat Crerand and Bobby Charlton. Benfica's consolation was an own goal by Shay Brennan. It was their first ever home defeat in the competition.

George with new tache and new motor (this time a Jag) in October 1967.

Jack Crompton, who always put a lot of thought into his training sessions during his years with Manchester United, checks George Best's pulse in February 1968. Jack, who had the chance of managing Luton in 1962 and had several other job offers, always preferred to stay at Old Trafford. He played a key role in the extra time 4–1 victory against Benfica in the European Cup Final at Wembley in 1968. A good quiz question: Who managed United after Dave Sexton and before Ron Atkinson? Jack Crompton. Jack, who died in 2013, also took a job coaching with the Sports Council at Manchester City's Platt Lane training centre.

▲ Mirror photographer Joe Bottomley came second in the sports category of the World Press Awards for this image taken at Old Trafford on 7 October 1967. The players flying through the air are, left to right, Paddy Crerand, Frank McLintock, George Best (amazing height gain for a small man) and John Radford. United won 1–0 with a goal from John Aston.

◀ Man-on-man defending seldom worked on George so Derby County decided they had a better chance with five (plus the referee) in the FA Cup third round match at the Baseball Ground on 22 January, 1966. It didn't do much good: United won 5-2 (Best 2, Denis Law 2 and David Herd).

● Like just about every young man in the world George Best dreamed of a home of his own and in 1968 asked an architect to build him this split-level house on Blossoms Lane, Bramhall, near Stockport. He called it Que Sera which may have been homage to his favourite holiday resort, Majorca, or an announcement that he doesn't really give a fuck. It certainly had nothing to do with Doris Day.

Que Sera came complete with a snooker table, sunken bath, underfloor heating, a subterranean garage for his Jag and a bar. The outcry in the national press was astonishing, the main objections being the bar (journalists don't drink of course) and that a 23-year-old footballer shouldn't own a £30k 'dream house'.

So Que Sera and George were trashed from the moment he moved in. One newspaper quoted an unnamed 'source' (aka a *Sun* reporter) and his claim that the neighbours had dubbed it a 'giant gents' toilet'.

In fact it was the sort of home many would aspire to – though no newspaper would ever admit that. It was a bit angular, but ahead of its time and still graces the design magazines of today. The problem

for George was that he was constantly besieged by fans and reporters and should have splashed out for a Berlin-type wall, electronic gates and CCTV cameras to surround the property (as the sports stars of today do).

He lasted three years there and after several breaches of club rules was soon back at Mrs Fullaway's in Aycliffe Avenue, Chorlton-cum-Hardy. This was taken in 1971.

A deserved Ballon d'Or for newly crowned European Footballer of the Year George Best. The ceremony took place after United's 2–0 league win over Burnley at Old Trafford on 19 April 1969. The two men getting in on the act are *L'Equipe* soccer writer Max Urbini and, in the background, chairman Louis Edwards.

Most Manchester United fans would never admit it but maybe those villains at Leeds were not as bad as we thought. For heaven's sake, they were actually family men with a sense of humour after all! Here some of the gang celebrate the Christmas of 1969 at Elland Road taking part in a donkey race with some of their children. Left to right: Goalkeeper David Harvey with his daughter Dawn, Billy Bremner with his son Billy, Johnny Giles with son Michael, Jack Charlton with Peter and Debbie, and Paul Reaney with daughter Paula.

● It's Elland Road on 6 September 1969 and another War of the Roses as the press liked to call it. Busby had retired (briefly) and Best (not for the first time) was claiming he was 'carrying the team on his own' (22 goals for him that season but eighth-place finish in the First Division under new manager Wilf McGuinness).

As for Leeds I can recall one fan telling me, in all seriousness just after George's death, that had he chosen Elland Road instead of Old Trafford he would still be alive.

Manager Don Revie 'never stood for shit' and would have kept the 'wayward genius' in check.

When I stopped laughing he added: 'George hated playing at Elland Road because (full-back) Paul Reaney never gave him a sniff.' I never saw that game so instead replied with this (possible apocryphal) story Best told of a Busby team-talk ahead of a game against Leeds in the 60s: 'Matt (obviously a Jock) went like this: "Gary Sprake, the goalkeeper . . . on his day a nasty piece of work. Right-back, Paul Reaney . . . dirty bastard. Left-back, Terry Cooper . . . even dirtier bastard. Johnny Giles . . . dirty little bastard. Centre-half, Jack Charlton . . . dirty big bastard. Right-half, wee Billy Bremner . . . good Scottish boy!"'

The United No.7 in the photograph is Best look-alike Willie Morgan and the Leeds players are, right to left, Norman 'Bite Yer Legs' Hunter, former Old Trafford starlet Johnny Giles and George's regular man-marker Paul Reaney, the full-back who 'never gave Best a sniff'. George scored both goals in the 2–2 draw.

That son of Gateshead Norman Hunter, who died of coronavirus in April 2020 was notoriously (and maybe unfairly) known as 'Bite Yer Legs Hunter' in his years as a feared defender with Leeds United. Here he shows a reluctant Jackie Charlton how to use his own legs as they celebrate his first England cap in 1965. It's doubtful a manager would allow such shenanigans these days!

The day after the 5-1 win against Benfica pictures like this were plastered all over the front and back pages of newspapers everywhere. George, his cool shades and sombrero had struck a chord and he was immediately nickname 'El Beatle'. Manchester United team-mates John Fitzpatrick (left) and David Herd look suitably impressed.

● At the height of the Swinging 60s George Best and good mate Mike Summerbee (Manchester City) ventured into the retail trade with the opening of an 'Edwardian' fashion boutique in Sale, south Manchester.

Initially it did well. The shop was besieged by potential buyers (mainly female) all hoping to catch a glimpse of Best (and possibly Summerbee). The financial side of the venture was run by Best's business manager Malcolm R. Mooney,

though Best did spend time in the business, mainly on Saturday mornings if Manchester United were at home.

Unfortunately, like sportsmen, fashion boutiques had a limited shelf-life, Summerbee got married and the Swinging 60s soon became the Un-swinging 70s and the business collapsed. The Sale site went first, closely followed by a branch they had opened at Cross Street in the city centre. United were relegated in 1974, Best's final season at the club.

Players are always at their happiest when training is over. Bobby Charlton is collared by a fan and his son in The Cliff car park, closely followed by, right to left: Nobby Stiles, George Best, John Aston and Brian Kidd. The straggler being rounded up by Jack Crompton is Paul Edwards who made a few first-team appearances in the 1969/70 season, including a spectacular strike against Manchester City in the League Cup semi-final.

A month after being sent off against Chelsea, George responded with a hat-trick against West Ham at Old Trafford on 18 September 1971. It was one of those days when he was impossible to handle . . . as defenders John McDowell (on the floor) and Billy Bonds were to find out.

By 1969 George had the world at his feet: he had inspired Manchester United to their first European Cup, had met a Danish fiancée called Eva Haradsted (no mean footballer herself) and bought a yellow Lotus Europa car. He was earning £2,000 per week for playing football (the national average then was £23) and there were extras: ghosted newspaper columns, the modelling, the endorsements and a new house. Like many of his girls and cars Eva and the Lotus didn't last long. She was involved in a serious car crash in Denmark and while she recovered Best had new models: another Scandinavian beauty called Siv Hederby . . . and an E-type Jag.

This was taken in Palma, Majorca, in the summer of 1969. The girl is actress Susan George, who was 19 at the time. There were several syndicated images of them posing together and all seemingly taken on the same day, 1 June: the couple cooling off in the sea, riding a pedalo, drinking in a seaside bar and dozens of Susan in a fetching bikini. The press described her as George's 'girlfriend', though there were no images of the couple together post-Majorca which one might expect. A cynic could argue that all this had been organised by Susan's publicist and it's true her career took off just after this (*Spring and Port Wine, Fright* and *Straw Dogs,* etc.) so let's just say for now the pair looked great together.

Discretion was never part of George Best's modus operandi and his girlfriends had to expect public scrutiny. Not that they ever complained. This is Janet McGregor greeting George at Manchester airport after his arrival from the club tour of America and Australia on 5 July 1967.

● This was a bit of a disaster for George and another example of his naivety and how easily he could be exploited. It never seemed to occur to him that a lot of the women he met had agendas of their own and that in many ways he was the conquest.

He had just walked out on Old Trafford in January, 1974, when newly crowned Miss World, Marjorie Wallace, a 19-year-old American from Indiana, turned up at his Slack Alice night club on Bottle Street, Manchester. It was a publicity stunt organised by a PR company and Ms Wallace stuck to the script: photos of the couple together by the bar, an exchange of phone calls and a promise to meet again.

Marjorie, like George, was no saint. She had had relationships with tennis star Jimmy Connors and the married Welsh tunesmith Tom Jones as well as a fiancé, the racing driver Peter Revson, who was also heir to the Revlon cosmetics fortune.

Where George fitted in to all this was easy to discover: a tour of his London haunts with Marjorie enjoying the limelight, lunch at San Lorenzo in Knightsbridge and Tramps night club in Piccadilly and, eventually, an arrest for allegedly stealing her fur coat, jewellery, handbag and passport. The case was eventually dismissed; Marjorie was dethroned by Miss World organisers when the Jones affair came to light. Just a few dull days in the life of George Best!

'What A Load of Cobblers' was the headline in one of the redtops after United's fifth round FA Cup win at Northampton's County Ground on 7 February 1970. It seemed harsh on a Third Division side – nicknamed the Cobblers after the town's long association with the shoe industry – and maybe the press should have done a play of words on Best's six goals, coming just after a six-week suspension. United needed a replay to see off Middlesbrough in the quarter-finals before the epic three-match semi-final defeat against Leeds (two sessions of extra time and an early goal from Billy Bremner).

'I Quit by George Best' was the front page headline of the *Sunday Mirror* on 21 May 1972. It goes without saying that the piece wasn't written by George . . . just presented in a way to look as though it had been written by George.

George and his first wife Angie were in London in September 1981 to promote one of his several autobiographies, this one being *Where Do I Go From Here?* This was a title almost as bad as the tedious, too-often-told anecdote that ends with the words: 'Where did it all go wrong, George?'

With second wife Alex in London's West End in May 2002.

With son, Calum, in 1997

In 1992 LWT produced a programme called *The Trouble with the Fifties*, presented by Michael Aspel and featuring, among others, Harry Secombe, Sylvia Syms and Lonnie Donegan. It was supposed to be a one-off special but because it was cheap and nostalgia was suddenly all the rage it soon begat *The Trouble with the Sixties*. It was launched on a rainy January day in 1993 with George and a BMW Isetta (these two presumably characteristic of 'trouble in the 60s') getting a push from disk jockeys Alan (Fluff) Freeman and Tony Blackburn, and Aspel.

● Seventeen months after being released by Manchester United Best was on the first of many comebacks, this one with Fourth Division Stockport County.

It was 10 November 1975; he was unfit and a bit above his fighting weight of around 69kg but still only 29 years old. He still put bums on seats, too, scoring from a 25-yard free kick in this friendly against Stoke City and delighting a crowd of 8,000. He had three games for Stockport before setting out an Odysseus-like journey that took in Cork, Los Angeles, Fulham, Fort Lauderdale, Edinburgh, San Jose, Bournemouth and Brisbane. 'I felt great, and am ready for the big time again,' he'd said after the Stockport match.

The famous (and infamous) pictured here at the launch of Bobby Moore's autobiography in October 1976: Elton John, Gerry Francis, Kenny Lynch, Jeff Powell of the *Daily Mail* (ghost writer with his own definition of the word 'ghost'), Jimmy Tarbuck, Bill Shankly (odd, given that his Anfield successor, Bob Paisley, loathed Powell and the *Mail* with a passion), Best, Moore and Joe Bugner.

It was December 2001 and another biography (*Blessed*) and another signing session. George looks a tad weary as he arrives in the much lamented Buchanan Street branch of Borders Books, Glasgow.

n 3 December 2005, George Best went home. Tens of thousands lined the streets of Belfast and the road to tormont Castle. Inset: A day after the funeral United fans of every age paid their tributes at Old Trafford.

Denis Law arrived at Huddersfield Town (manager Bill Shankly) as a bespectacled, squinty-eyed 16-year-old in 1956. Fifteen years later he was back at Leeds Road to score a 73rd minute goal in a 3–0 win. The other goals came from Charlton and Best . . . the last time all three scored in the same match.

Twenty-year-old Denis Law takes on Harry Gregg and defenders Maurice Setters and Noel Cantwell (on only his seventh appearance for United after his transfer from West Ham) at Old Trafford on the last day of 1960. It was Law's first of two spells with City and it wasn't long before he was off to Torino and was the holder of another British transfer record (£110,000). A year later the Lawman was back at Manchester (United).

● Denis Law and former Hibbee Joe Baker pose with Turin sporting director Gigi Peronace on their arrival in Italy in the summer of 1961.

The maximum wage rule was still in force at home and the temptation of lire was too great for some (John Charles in 1957 was soon followed by Jimmy Greaves and Gerry Hitchen).

Law and Baker were greeted like film stars, but Torino, rather like Manchester United nine years later, was still suffering from the effects of a terrible tragedy. In 1949 all members of Serie A's all-conquering Il Grande Torino were killed in an air crash high above the city and club and fans were still recovering.

Law didn't like the defensive tactics employed by virtually every team in Italy, was kicked black and blue and by the middle of 1962 he was heading back to Manchester.

It's 23 April 1968 and Sir Matt and Denis Law are taking this one seriously. Matt had even come out of his office and on to the Old Trafford pitch to prepare his side for the European Cup semi-final first leg match against Real Madrid next day. United won 1–0 with a George Best goal but Law was injured in the match and not only missed the second leg, but the final, too.

● Here we go again! Denis Law checks Brian Kidd's passport ahead of the flight from Ringway to Buenos Aires where United were to take on Estudiantes for the World Club Championship. The other players are Francis Burns and Willie Morgan and maybe they should all have stayed at home. Estudiantes and Argentina as a whole obviously hadn't forgotten the '66 World Cup when England manager Sir Alf Ramsey had called them 'animals'.

Sir Alf had it half right because Estudiantes turned out to be the dirtiest team in history. Nobby Stiles had been targeted from the start with kicks, punches and a head-butt and almost inevitably he retaliated and was sent off.

The return match at Old Trafford wasn't much better, with George Best getting the red card this time. Willie Morgan got a consolation goal in the 90th minute. Estudiantes represented South America in the cup for the next two years . . . and, I'm happy to say, lost both . . . to AC Milan and Feyenoord.

▶ Happy landings at Ringway in July 1967 for Denis Law and Brian Kidd after arriving back from Manchester United's tour of America and Australia. They had flown out only four days after being crowned champions for the seventh time and all in the cause of filthy lucre. In America they lost to Benfica and Dundee but did better in New Zealand, beating local sides in Auckland and Christchurch (8–1 and 11–0). In Australia United scored 33 goals and won seven of the eight games.

▲ On the afternoon of Saturday, 27 April 1974 United were minutes away from relegation so little wonder manager Tommy Docherty looks so desperate. Paddy Crerand manages a smile for the camera, but his days as assistant manager at Old Trafford were numbered too, for Docherty soon sacked him with a combination of Frank Blunstone and Tommy Cavanagh taking over.

▲ Manchester United manager Tommy Docherty, Denis Law and David Sadler ruminate in the dressing room after the 1–1 draw against Leeds United at Old Trafford on 22 December 1972. By the following summer, Law had spent 11 years at Old Trafford and scored 237 goals in 404 games . . . but Busby was no longer in charge. Docherty decided he was surplus to requirements and Law heard the news while drinking in an Aberdeen pub that he was to join Manchester City on a free transfer. It gave him (reluctantly because he had been ready to retire) a chance to extend his career . . . for United at least, a big mistake!

● Local derbies have always been emotional affairs, but at some stage in the early '70s passion turned into sheer hatred, particularly at the Maine Road end of town where one player regarded defeating Manchester United as a personal crusade.

It wasn't always thus: with Old Trafford decimated by the Luftwaffe 'home' games were at Maine Road for four years. This wasn't the heresy it may seem now: Busby had played for City and many of his Manchester United players had grown up in Blue-supporting families. My father, a passionate Red, often went to Maine Road if United were away, mainly because we didn't have a car and couldn't afford the travel expenses. But he also liked football per se and it didn't depend on the colour of the jerseys.

I wasn't particularly fond of City. Captain Tony Book and his rolled-up sleeves used to infuriate me, and the basic pessimism of most City supporters was just as bad, but never to the extent of actually hating them. The first player quoted in that fashion was Mike Doyle of Manchester City. Some of his colleagues at Maine Road – notably Lee, Tueart and Summerbee

– pretended to despise anything in Red but they were just wind-up merchants; Doyle's hatred came from deep within and it's hard to understand even now.

Doyle, a defender people like to describe as 'committed' (his autobiography was titled *Blue Blood*) did a lot of hating. He hated George Best dating back, apparently, to United's win over City in an FA Youth Cup semi-final in 1964. Doyle had a chance to get rid of some of his ire on 27 April 1974, when City won 1–0 at Old Trafford and a United team containing Best were relegated (though the result was immaterial as fellow strugglers Birmingham beat Norwich City 2–1 on the same day).

It was a day replete in the sort of irony common in sport. The winning goal came from Denis Law, appearing in a Blue jersey for the first time in 13 years.

Birmingham City were managed at the time by Freddie Goodwin, one of the original Busby Babes. After Law's goal and a predictable pitch invasion, Book wisely substituted him and the game was abandoned. The result stood and Denis retired four months later. Doyle died from liver failure in June 2011.

◀ **Law was in no mood to celebrate his back-heel goal that gave Manchester City the 1–0 victory at Old Trafford. Goalkeeper Alex Stepney is dumfounded, as are team-mates Alex Forsyth, Stewart Houston, Jim Holton, Martin Buchan and Brian Greenhoff. City's Dennis Tueart is happy.**

A goal (past Gordon Banks no less) and an FA Cup winner's medal for Denis Law after the 3–1 defeat of Leicester City at Wembley on 25 May 1963. It became a golden era for Law and United with Denis scoring 46 goals in one season and receiving the European Footballer of the Year award the year after.

The Scotland line-up that faced Northern Ireland in the Home Championships (remember that) on 8 November 1960. Scotland won 5-2 at Hampden Park the next day with goals from Ralph Brand (2), Alex Young, Denis Law and an Eric Caldow penalty. Left to right, back: manager Ian McColl, Duncan MacKay, Dave Mackay, John Plenderleith, Lawrie Leslie, Jim Baxter, Eric Caldow, Jimmy Millar, Dawson Walker (trainer). Front row: George Herd, Denis Law, Alex Young, Ralph Brand, Davie Wilson.

A belated press call for the European Cup winners at Old Trafford on 25 July 1968 . . . two months after the final; Denis Law was injured and missed Wembley . . . though you wouldn't think so. Best and some of the others looks as though they have just returned from a funeral.

Training was primitive in the '70s but sportsmen still needed support, particularly when injured. Denis had missed most of the 1969/70 season, but there was always advice from assistant manager Jimmy Murphy to fall back on. Murphy was more mentor than coach by then and his time at Old Trafford was soon over. Busby had retired (temporarily) and new head coach Wilf McGuinness wanted changes (including, bizarrely, placing Law on the transfer list). Next in the hot seat was Cork's own Frank O'Farrell who didn't fare much better. Law, by all accounts, then recommended Tommy Docherty who responded by transfer listing Law again, City stepped in and the rest, as they say, is history.

Pat Crerand tries to play the peace- maker during the 2–1 win against Blackpool at Bloomfield Road on 14 November 1964. No chance: hard-line referee Peter Rhodes has already made up his mind and Denis has to make the Walk of Shame. Rhodes' other famous victim during his 20 years as a referee was Liverpool's Ian St John, of *Saint and Greavesie*. The other United players here are Tony Dunne (right) and David Herd. The Blackpool player is Leslie Lea.

A lone bobby escorts Denis Law to Sheffield's Victoria Station after the beaks of the FA Disciplinary Committee had handed him a four-week suspension. He had been accused of abusive language, with referee Peter Rhodes insisting the player had called him a c..t after he had booked him for a foul on Blackpool's Alan Ball. Denis (and witness Pat Crerand) insisted the word he had used was 'coot' (a small water bird). It surprised no one when Denis lost his appeal.

The ultimate family man: Denis at home in Bowden, Cheshire, in September 1973 with wife Diana (together for over 50 years as I write this now) and boys Gary (9), Andrew (7), Robert (5) and Iain (3). A girl, also Diana, arrived in January 1974.

Law once famously said of Manchester United manager Frank O'Farrell that 'he came and went a stranger', which seemed unfair, given that O'Farrell had to cope with George Best and Matt Busby who was alleged to have retired, but actually hadn't (even attempting to keep his old office). There were some happy times for the O'Farrell family in July 1971, when Ann and the kids had tea and toast with Paddy Crerand and Denis in the 'office canteen'.

Who are those two guys with Denis Law and Mike Summerbee? A couple of nobodies called Xi Jinping (President of China) and David Cameron (Prime Minister of the UK) that's who. This summit meeting took place at Manchester City Academy in City's Etihad Campus on Xi's last day of a state visit on 23 October 2015. I would love to have listened to that lady translator as she coped with Aberdonian and Mandarin at the same time.

These three men sure knew the path to goal: Tom Finney, Denis Law and Nat Lofthouse in April 1990 at the launch of Soccaball, a project to improve skills for youngsters.

● A contacts book has always been fundamental to the job of a journalist. I have four complete notebooks, dating back to the '60s and I wasn't even a reporter in those days. Most of the numbers and addresses are worthless now but out of interest, and the writing of this book, I checked my list dating back to my 11 years with Express Newspapers in Manchester.

In those days addresses and phone numbers were often swapped, everyone knowing that you are unlikely to use them but equipped if you do. There is all sorts of exotica ranging, in alphabetical order, from Atkinson (Ron) and Arum (Bob) to Yorkshire TV and Yates Wine Bar, all of which seem to symbolize life on a national newspaper in the '70s. I found the relevant L on the same page as Lloyd (Clive), Lorimer (Peter) and Lumley (Joanna) and, 45 years after I had last spoken to him

and purely out of curiosity, I rang 0161 928 .... and asked for Denis. 'He doesn't live here anymore,' said the very affable lady who answered before adding: 'We get calls for him all the time.' I asked the obvious question: why not change the number? She didn't hesitate: 'Oh, we couldn't do that!' So the King lives on, even in posh Altrincham.

Like the other members of the Three Musketeers Law has had his setbacks to which he has always responded as one would expect: he became patron of the Meningitis Now charity after his son Andrew almost died from the disease in 1992 and had to go through his own surgery for prostate cancer in 2003. He remains today an active and high profile supporter of several charities and why he has never been knighted remains a mystery. To me at least.

aestro was a BBC2 series written by the late Frank Keating, who I still regard as one of the greatest of sporting wordsmiths. The series ran from 1981 to 1985 and the format was simple: Keating meets a famous sportsman (no women, if I remember rightly) who reminisces about his career with support from archive footage. It was the sort of thing the BBC used to do very well and Keating had always excelled with sporty nostalgia. Meeting him was, according to David Gower, 'a gentle pleasure' and even Lester Piggott found it hard to resist the congeniality of that West Country lilt. Keating got the best out of Bobby Charlton – a maestro in many senses of the word – but a man often seen as stern, unsmiling and always measured in his responses.

One former Busby Babe who knew Charlton well suggested to me that 'Bob was terrified a camera might catch him smiling' particularly at the various Munich ceremonies he was virtually obliged to attend.

Keating's interview was a delight: a relaxed Bobby at home in Knutsford, Bobby with his wife Norma, Bobby with daughters Suzanne (some time before her days as a BBC weather forecaster) and Andrea, their horses . . . and Bobby with smiles all round. Some elements of the conversation were predictable . . . until we got to footage of one of his most famous moments, England's first goal against Mexico in the 1966 World Cup at Wembley. Charlton, as we all know, picked up the ball in his own half, found space to run, cut inside and let fly from around 30 yards. I marvelled, not only at Charlton's speed and control but the ability to shoot with his wrong foot (he was left-handed) and find the exact spot.

The goalkeeper couldn't get near it. It was a shock then, 17 years later, when Charlton said to Keating: 'It's the old

Pals for life Sir Bobby Charlton and Kaiser Franz Beckenbauer get together at the England training camp in Navacerrada, Madrid, in June 1982. It was the day before the World Cup Group B clash between their two countries and 16 years after they had faced each other in the final at Wembley. Franz and Bobby still argue (in the friendliest way) about a famous/infamous Geoff Hurst goal and an infamous/famous Russian linesman.

Charlton (close by the door) with the England squad at London airport on 19 June 1958 after being knocked out of the World Cup in Stockholm. England had been badly weakened by the Munich disaster.

Roger Byrne, Tommy Taylor and Duncan Edwards had been certain selections for Sweden; David Pegg had won his first England cap the previous year and Eddie Colman and Mark Jones could soon have joined him.

As Geoffrey Green of *The Times* wrote: 'England's hopes of winning the World Cup suffered a blow when the flower of Manchester United lay tragically scattered in the snow of Munich Airport last Thursday. Those same hopes took another jolt on Saturday when the organising committee of FIFA assembled in Stockholm to make the draw for the final stages of the World Cup competition. England did well to hold eventual winners Brazil to a 0-0 draw before losing to the second-seeded Soviet Union in a play-off.'

The players are, left to right: Derek 'The Tank' Kevan (a centre-forward still beloved by fans at West Bromwich Albion and Manchester City), Bill Slater of Wolves, West Brom's Don Howe, Peter Brabrook (Chelsea) and in the background Peter Broadbent (also Wolves).

Jimmy Murphy in me. Don't aim at a specific part of the goal, just get it on target.' Like many I had always been convinced that a Charlton goal was the football equivalent of a guided missile! It was also clear how crucial Murphy had been to the young players at Old Trafford down the years.

By rights Charlton should have followed his uncle Jackie Milburn to Newcastle United, but mother Cissie, by all accounts, was charmed by the winning combination of Busby and Murphy on a visit to Ashington. He was 15 and fresh out of school when he arrived in Manchester. In his early days he played on the left wing, occasionally at inside-forward, but it was in the deep-lying centre-forward role he is best remembered along with that explosive shooting – 249 goals in 758 games for United – astute passing and a formidable work rate.

By 1971, however, it was clear that the star was on the wane. He had never played for England again after being controversially substituted in the 1970 World Cup quarter-final against Germany in Leon and 12 months later he was 34, the pace had gone, along with most of the hair.

His then manager, Tommy Docherty, faced a tough choice, and one that Busby had been unwilling to confront (though Docherty's predecessor Frank O'Farrell had had no such problems). In the end Charlton made his own decision.

There were less gilded arenas. He tried management with Preston – for whom he turned out as a player in 1974, the year he was awarded the CBE – and later became a director at Wigan Athletic, both with a depressing lack of success. But he did return to United as a member of the football board in 1994, the year he was knighted.

Today he is not only the last Munich survivor among the players, but an adored sportsman worldwide, a figurehead for the club and football as a whole and a link with the game's past, present and future.

World War Three breaks out on 27 March 1965, as Leeds United and Manchester United meet to sort out the FA Cup semi-final at Hillsborough. Pat Crerand gets a grip of little innocent Billy Bremner as Bobby Charlton tries to play the honest broker, Bobby's big brother Jack and Denis Law (his shirt already ripped) square up, while Leeds captain Bobby Collins takes over as referee. It finished 0–0; Leeds won the replay 1–0 (a Bremner goal!) but lost in the final to Liverpool. Manchester United had already clinched the First Division title.

A double for Bobby Charlton in the 2–1 derby win at Maine Road on 30 September 1967. Denis Law and George Best celebrate; the City players are Glyn Pardoe, Mike Doyle (new haircut), skipper Tony Book and goalkeeper Ken Mulhearn. City had the last laugh, of sorts, winning at Old Trafford in the return fixture and in May 1968 lifting the First Division title for the first time in three decades. Unfortunately for all at Maine Road the achievement was lost amid the celebrations of United's European Cup win 18 days later.

● Even Jimmy Greaves can't believe his eyes as Bobby Charlton is booked for time-wasting during the FA Charity Shield match at Old Trafford on 12 August 1967.

The game finished 3–3 and the players, left to right, are: Charlton, Greaves, George Best, Denis Law (with ball), Nobby Stiles (angry), Brian Kidd, Dave Mackay (6) and Terry Venables (10).

It was said to have been Charlton's only booking (later rescinded by the referee) though it was discovered some 30 years later that both Bobby and brother Jackie were cautioned during England's hot-blooded World Cup win against Argentina in the 1966 World Cup.

The referee, Rudolf Kreitlein, was German; few of the Argentinians spoke English so there were linguistic difficulties.

It was only in 1998, when Charlton was at a FIFA conference on fair play that he discovered he had been cautioned during the '66 match. Someone had gone into the FIFA archive and found the match report: Charlton had been trying to play the peacemaker and his intervention had been misunderstood (though the booking stayed).

The only positive thing about the whole affair (apart from the Argentine captain being sent off and England winning 1–0) was that the first red and yellow cards appeared in time for the 1970 World Cup where they were much needed.

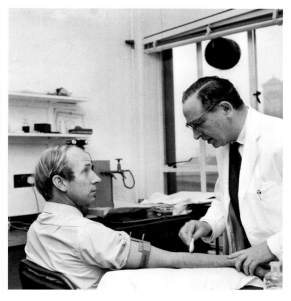

As part of England's build-up for the 1970 Mexico World Cup, the players had to undergo blood tests at St Mary's Hospital. An apprehensive Bobby Charlton takes his turn.

Charlton clears the windows of his S-type at The Cliff ahead of the FA Cup meeting with Northampton on 9 February 1970.

Three-year-old Suzanne Charlton watched by 15-month-old Andrea takes another call for her dad at the family home in Flixton. England had just won the World Cup against West Germany at Wembley and the telephone had gone non-stop. Within a day Bobby had enough and set off 'anywhere' to escape the pandemonium. 'We wanted to be with ourselves,' Charlton said later. 'The phone started ringing first thing this morning and hasn't stopped since.'

England players have time on their hands at their base in Hendon on 10 July 1966, with the start of the World Cup one day away. Left to right: Alan Ball, Ian Callaghan, Geoff Hurst, Roger Hunt, Bobby and Jackie.

Five years after disaster Manchester United are back on the trophy trail, here celebrating the 3–1 defeat of Leicester at Wembley on 25 May 1963: full-back Tony Dunne, Bobby Charlton, captain Noel Cantwell, Pat Crerand, Albert Quixall, David Herd (two goals with the other coming from Denis Law) and Johnny Giles. Nobby Stiles is just visible behind him.

Two months after Wembley and with another new season ahead it was back to work for the Manchester United squad. Among the players are Charlton and David Sadler (weight training), Alan Gowling (far left), Brian Kidd, Shay Brennan and John Aston, man of the match against Benfica. Leading the training is United's goalkeeping legend Jack Crompton another Wembley winner in 1948 when Manchester United won the FA Cup and gave Matt Busby his first title.

The 1970 World Cup finals in Mexico turned into a disaster for England with captain Bobby Moore accused of stealing a bracelet from a jewellery shop in Bogota, supersaver Gordon Banks laid low by a stomach bug before the quarter-final against West Germany and Charlton substituted by Alf Ramsey just when he had the Germans and Franz Beckenbauer under control. Before that there was some relaxation for a confident England side by the hotel swimming pool in Leon: Moore, Jack Charlton, Martin Peters, Colin Bell, Roger Hunt and Bobby.

▶ Weren't they supposed to be rivals, enemies even? Not in the eyes of Bobby Charlton who helped open the furniture business of Manchester City captain Tony Book in 1970. Forever smiley City manager Joe Mercer looks on.

▲ Denis Law and Bobby Charlton swap shirts after the British Championship match at Wembley on 10 April 1965. It had ended in a 2–2 draw with both of the Manchester United colleagues scoring a goal apiece.

Almost everyone, anywhere, wanted to be Bobby Charlton . . . even folk in Barnsley. In the Ken Loach film *Kes* the wonderful Brian Glover played a dysfunctional games master (we can all remember them) who organised a match with his class and announced: 'It's Manchester United versus Spurs in this important fifth-round Cup tie here at Old Trafford and it's the fair-haired, slightly balding Charlton to kick off.' His goalkeeper, played by the 14-year-old David Bradley, had no interest in football . . . or even Bobby Charlton.

Bobby Charlton and Nat Lofthouse – the Lion of Vienna and Bolton Wanderers finest – pay their floral tributes on the 50th anniversary.

When you move into your 70s you tend to spend a lot of time at funerals, as Sir Bobby knows better than most. This was the service for Sir Henry Cooper at The Corpus Christi Church at Tonbridge, Kent on 18 May 2011. Among others paying tribute were Kevin Kegan and Cliff Morgan, the famed Welsh rugby player, broadcaster and programme-maker. Two years later Cliff had gone, too.

This is a replica of the original Munich plaque. It stood by the main entrance to the directors' box until development, notably a brand-new 'megastore', forced its move. The whereabouts of the original remains a mystery.

GORDON AIN'T A MORON

In 2004 I went to see Gordon Taylor in his offices just off Oxford Street in the centre of Manchester. At the time Taylor was at the height of his power as head of the Professional Footballers' Association (PFA) and the richest union official in Britain. I was there to ask about the Munich testimonial fund of 1998, how it was organised and who, if any, had benefitted.

It was a remarkable couple of hours. Taylor arrived half an hour late in a Mercedes the size of a small tank, his staff were, almost exclusively, comely, welcoming ladies in their 40s and dressed to kill, as they say. At 1pm precisely everyone – Taylor and ladies included – left for lunch, leaving me alone. Taylor had said I could examine all the files involving the Munich air crash but 'you mustn't take any away'. He didn't say I wasn't allowed to copy them, which I did.

It was heart-rending stuff. There were begging letters from relatives of the dead crew, passengers and some of the journalists, all of which had been sent to Martin Edwards (still United CEO at the time). Edwards had simply passed these on to Taylor.

'There were a number of applications from other people, including relatives of the dead journalists,' he confirmed once he got back from lunch. 'I had to tell them that because we were the PFA the fund could only apply to players and their dependants The terms of the benefit and who would be entitled to shares had been decided and published in advance. It's sad, but that's the way it is.'

A testimonial match finally went ahead at Old Trafford on 18 August 1998, featuring a Manchester United XI against a European XI and involving Eric Cantona, who was to get most of the receipts. Some £1m was left and divided among survivors and families of the dead players. Quite naturally, given that the Eric Cantona Show had taken over a match intended to remember Munich, the anger and bitterness lasts to this day.

Harry Gregg had demanded at the time: 'I wanted to

see gate receipts, sale of programmes; they had to forward all receipts of money going out. I said I realised that for 40 years Manchester United FC never wanted to accept the Munich tragedy as part of their lives; maybe the PLC would like to make up for the shortcomings of their predecessors. Some people there did help in their own small way. But it took two years to pay it out.'

John Doherty, who with Taylor, the late sports writer David Meek and head of the Manchester United Former Players Association David Sadler had done much to organise the occasion, was just as rancorous when I met him not long after the Taylor interview.

'Someone asked me "what was your aim" and I said it was to raise a million and we did that,' he said. 'I thought we did a very good job. As for thanks, I think the club got three or four letters, I didn't receive one. I'm not sure about Gordon.

'The thing that has always hurt me is that not one of those players I played with took the trouble to either pick up the phone to me or just drop me a card to say thank you. By the end I was sick of it. There were even some people who thought that the ones that died shouldn't get anything, just the ones living; and why not Matt's family? They were just as entitled as anyone else. Matt Busby had been injured in the crash after all. When you get down to it you have to be harsh and say that players like Jackie (Blanchflower) and Johnny (Berry) had their careers ended by injury, just like me. But if someone came to me tomorrow and asked if I would do it again, I would probably say yes.'

Former Busby Babe turned manager Freddie Goodwin looks on in approval as Gordon Taylor signs on for Birmingham City in December 1970. Taylor, a winger, also played for Bury, Bolton and Blackpool ('all the Bs' as he liked to put it).

WHO DID YOU THINK YOU WERE KIDDING, MISTER HITLER?

Manchester, its twin Salford and its citizens had suffered horribly in the Second World War. As one of the largest industrialised centres in Europe it had been a Luftwaffe target almost from the beginning of the war. When night fell of 22 December 1940, bombers dropped 272 tons of high explosives and 2,000 incendiary bombs. Over a 24-hour period 30 acres were destroyed within a mile of Manchester Town Hall, flattened 50,000 homes and erased famous landmarks, including the Free Trade Hall and the Victoria Buildings.

On 11 March 1941, the bombers were back, this time targeting the Port of Manchester and Trafford Park, home to the munitions factory of Vickers and Ford, builders of Rolls Royce engines.

The job that faced Busby when he arrived at Old Trafford seemed like a microcosm of Britain: insolvent, derelict and,

Old Trafford had never been a target for the Luftwaffe, but it was thought that the crew of a Heinkel 111 crew, mindful of the need to get rid of payload, landed their last stick on the football ground on Warwick Road North. Four years later this was the sight that greeted Busby on his first day at work. Grass grew on the terraces, there were no floodlights and a Nissen hut on the south stand was to serve as the players' dressing rooms. For the next four years home games had to be played at Maine Road, the home of Manchester City.

Plain Matt Busby pictured in his Liverpool FC kit in 1936. Like hundreds of others his football career was interrupted by war and when Company Sergeant Major Matt Busby of the Ninth Battalion of the King's Liverpool Regiment was demobbed he was 36. He had little experience of management.

as he soon found out, with a workforce whose best years, like Busby himself, had been lost. Busby was to produce three great sides in three different eras and of three differing styles, though each a blueprint for the next: cost-nothing locals, trained apprentices and one or two shrewd buy-ins. This is usually seen as the nucleus of the first, runners-up in the league for the first two years after the war and FA Cup winners (4–2 over Blackpool at Wembley) in April, 1948.

Busby's youngsters were ready. The late Jimmy Armfield, the former Blackpool and England player, and a regular in the *Daily Express* offices in Ancoats Street when I worked there, saw the nucleus of the Babes when playing for Blackpool Reserves in the old Central League.

He recalled: 'Bobby Charlton, Eddie Colman, David Pegg, Albert Scanlon, Mark Jones and Geoff Bent were all in the team, which shows how good they were at the time.

'United were attracting all the best schoolboys, but the thing that stuck most in my mind was the incredible crowd, around 26,000 at Old Trafford. Blackpool had a fair side and we always used to try and win the Central League but there wasn't much chance with that sort of opposition.'

Growing up in north Manchester we always thought of the '50s team as celebrities but celebrities with a common touch. The names were ordinary: David, Mark, Geoff, Duncan, Eddie. Roger, Tommy and Billy (Liam but renamed by fans).

'Hold on for your given name as long you can because for sure they'll be calling you something else soon,' said club captain and countryman John (Jackie in Mancunian parlance) on the day Liam arrived at Old Trafford.

It has always been hard to define 'Busby Babe' (a name invented by a sports writer and one that Busby hated). The

And a merry Christmas to you, too. Left: what was left of the Free Trade Hall in Peter Street on 23 December 1940. Right: As is usual in wars, the bombing was quite indiscriminate.

The title-winning season of 1951/52 proved to be the swansong for many of Busby's players. By the time of United's away match at Huddersfield on 31 October 1953 there had already been first-team debuts for 18-year-old Jackie Blanchflower and 21-year-old Roger Byrne. At Huddersfield Busby fielded seven under the age of 22. It was an undistinguished 0-0 draw but the Busby Babes were born. One of the first, Albert Scanlon, seen training here with Allenby Chilton in 1954, said: 'Matt saw the writing on the wall for a lot of the old guard and the kids started coming in.'

July 1957 and Tommy Taylor leads the way in training.

Eddie Colman and Dennis Viollet lead the way off the Hillsborough pitch after the 2–0 FA Cup semi-final win over Birmingham on 23 March 1957. Shaking hands is Duncan Edward, and David Pegg faces a one-fan pitch invasion. Big Mark Jones can just be seen in the far distance.

obituaries of Ray Wood and Johnny Berry, who made their debuts in the early '50s, invariably grouped them as Busby Babes, but in fact they were bought in: Wood from Darlington and Berry from Birmingham City.

'Tommy Taylor was not a Babe, either,' John Doherty, the former Manchester United inside-forward would insist. 'You had to be born in Manchester, or reared by the club. Mark Jones was from Yorkshire, but he was a Babe; Jackie Blanchflower was Irish and he was a Babe. Jeff Whitefoot was a Babe and is still one of the youngest to play for United at 16. Him, Brian Birch, Bob Birkett, an outside-right who played for England schoolboys, Mark Jones, they were really the first of them, Jackie Blanchflower, then Dave Pegg and me; Foulkesy (Bill Foulkes) the following year.'

Doherty was, therefore, a Busby Babe by definition: 'Matt and Jimmy were very choosy about who they brought in. I was born in Stretford and went to United in 1949 as a schoolboy. I was an illegal signing because I hadn't finished school. Jeff Whitefoot was in the office and I joined him there, answering the phone, helping the office staff with bits and pieces and training in the morning.'

● People may snigger at the clumsy orchestration but at least the photographer left us a memory that will be frozen in time. A lot of young players lodged with Mrs Watson on Talbot Road close by the cricket ground.

Meals were served around a communal table, some – although not all – helped with the washing-up and bedrooms were shared. Mrs Watson had a black-and-white telly in the lounge which helped ward off the inevitable effects of home-sickness.

From bottom left and working clockwise round to bottom right: Tommy Taylor, Mrs Watson, Bobby Charlton, Liam Whelan, Winnie, Jackie Blanchflower, Mark Jones, Gordon Clayton, Joan,

Alan Rhodes and Duncan Edwards. It was taken in September 1953, a far cry from homes in million-pound bunkers in Cheshire's golden triangle, with iron gates and CCTV cameras to keep the public at bay.

Whenever I think of sport today I remember Ridley Scott's famous quote, referring to film-making but just as applicable to footballers: 'Never let yourself be seen in public unless they pay for it.'

I cling on to my Manchester United fan base alright and hope they win on a regular basis but wouldn't lose sleep if they didn't. If a member of the current first-team squad turned up at my front door dressed in training kit I would struggle to tell him from a council bin man.

CAPTAIN, M

Y CAPTAIN

y 1958 and with his 29th birthday approaching Roger Byrne was already planning for the future he wasn't going to have. Byrnes could be said to have been comfortably off but unlike many before or since, he was well aware that he couldn't play for ever. His salary for 1957, for example, comprised a basic wage of £744, plus bonuses. His newspaper column in the *Manchester Evening News* and several minor sponsorships, including a Raleigh bicycle endorsement, were dependant on him being a well-known sportsman and of that he was well aware. He enrolled for a degree course in physiotherapy, his chosen career post-football. He also met his future wife, Joy Cooper, when both were studying at a local hospital.

'We met as students,' Joy said during a lengthy and emotional interview with her and her son Roger Jnr in 2003. Joy had remarried to James Worth, a former schoolteacher, but was willing to reminisce about the man she had lost in Germany (as was Mr Worth).

'There was an intake of students and we knew one of them played football. 'None of us knew any names at United and City and we looked at all these chaps and thought: "Which one is it?" Roger actually attended in the afternoons after training in the morning. We went out after the hospital ball at a local hospital and that was it,'

◀ **PREVIOUS PAGE**
Manchester United,
unlike members of the
Football Association,
never saw Europe as 'here
be dragons' territory.
Here Roger, with David
Pegg, Jackie Blanchflower
and Tommy Taylor close
by, signs an autograph
for a young Madrid fan
before the first leg of the
European Cup semi-
final in April 1957. The
home team were not
so welcoming and this
was a harsh lesson for
Busby's young side.
United lost 3–1 (goals
from Rial, Di Stefano and
Mateos and a reply by
Taylor) but United were,
as *The Guardian* put it,
kicked from penalty box
to post as the Spaniards
elbowed their way to
victory. The home leg
was drawn 2–2 but there
was condolence in the
knowledge that Dennis
Viollet (9) and Taylor
(8) were top scorers in
the tournament as a
whole. Ten years later
came revenge in another
European Cup semi-
final against Real and,
at last, a final victory at
Wembley.

she said. 'I soon finished up going to the home matches
and the local away matches, usually with Roger's best
man, John Pickles. The wives were treated as any other
supporter. After games I waited till Roger came out to
the car park.'

There were more eye-catching players at Old Trafford – Taylor with his goalscoring, Colman with his
jinking, Edwards with everything – but Byrne remains
my favourite. I admired his calmness under pressure,
his calculating football brain and what would be seen
as 'professionalism' today – 'Booed Byrne Just Loved
It' screamed a *Daily Mirror* headline above a report of
a Manchester derby in 1957. He was a different man
off the field. 'The nicest fellow who ever walked God's
earth,' said Harry Gregg.

Fans can be quite provincial when choosing their
champions, too. Roger was a Mancunian, which has
always dictated my judgement. Right or wrong, I'll defend
anyone born in the same little corner of Manchester:
Danny Boyle, the Neville brothers, George Ford, his dad
Mike, Iestyn Harris. I know nothing about the film career
of Anna Friel but she was born in Rochdale so that was
good enough for me. I even tried some Morrissey pieces
on YouTube once, having convinced myself that anyone
born in Davyhulme can't be all that bad.

Harry Gregg, who could be quite dogmatic about
things like this, insisted that Roger, Albert Scanlon,
Dennis Viollet, Geoff Bent and Eddie Colman were the
'heart of United – because they were really Manchester
Busby Babes' (Colman and Bent were from Salford
which, as any Salfordian will tell you, is a different city
altogether).

Roger also put me in mind of another childhood
hero, Wilson the Wonder Athlete, the star of the comic
book *The Wizard*, a man taciturn, quiet by nature, but
capable of amazing feats of strength and endurance. He
climbed Everest long before Hillary and Tensing and

Stanley
Matthews,
the wizard of
dribble, excels
himself in ball
control, as in
full flight he
'stands' on the
ball to fox Roger
Byrne, United's
international
full-back who is
reserve for the
big game.

Cheeky, extrovert and in playing terms generous (only two goals in the whole of his United career) and a young Salfordian bound for greatness. Eddie Colman training at The Cliff on 1 May 1957, three days ahead of the FA Cup Final against Aston Villa at Wembley. The newspaper picture desk reversed the image by mistake. Bobby Charlton is 01!

● It's 21 April 1956 and another trophy for Roger and his jubilant team-mates after the 1–0 win over Portsmouth at Old Trafford. Scorer Dennis Viollet is in the No.10 jersey and Duncan Edwards is next to him. Matt Busby is in the crowd behind them.

Roger Byrne and United were to take a back-to-back title in 1957 ... but the club had to wait another eight years for the next. The season-long tussle with Leeds from 1964 to '65 went to goal difference (amazingly, United were more curmudgeonly in defence that year) and the Yorkies could only manage a 3–3 draw against Birmingham on the last day. Busby's team was to finish runners-up to Burnley the following year (those were the days!) but landed the title again the following year.

The season saw Denis Law in his pomp (23 goals) and the team went unbeaten from December 1966 to May the following year. The cup was handed over after the stunning 6–1 win at West Ham. Unfortunately, this was the last hardware for another 26 years.

guided England to an Ashes win over Australia, which in Byrne's case might not have been fictional.

'It was touch and go whether Roger played cricket or football,' said Joy, 'and he was also a good golfer and boxer. He was good at every sport, in fact. I loved ice skating and used to go regularly with a crowd from the hospital to the Ice Palace. He wasn't supposed to go, but we dragged him along one time. He had never skated before and he just put the boots on and off he went; it really annoyed everyone. We kept saying "for goodness sake, don't fall over" but he never did.'

It was one of Busby's wee army of scouts, Joe Armstrong, who first recognised the promise of the 15-year-old schoolboy in a Lancashire Amateur League fixture in 1948. Byrne and a Ryder Brow Jnrs team-mate, a winger

Fans pay their last tribute to Roger Byrne ahead of the service at Flixton Parish Church in February 1958. He was later cremated at Blackley cemetery.

called Brian Statham, were offered amateur forms. Byrne accepted, Statham stuck to other sporting love, cricket.

Roger's remarkable pace made him a natural winger initially, but it was a position he despised. He could also be 'an awkward bugger' according to Matt Busby's son, Sandy: 'Roger fell out with my dad at the end of his first season, 1951/52. He wanted an increase in bonuses and didn't like playing at outside-left. He wasn't happy at all and one time asked for a transfer.'

When he was moved to full-back he blossomed, as his 275 first-team appearances and 33 for his country show. According to former England team-mate, Jimmy Armfield, the loss of Byrne, Duncan Edwards and Tommy Taylor struck the national side a blow from which it took almost a decade to recover and 'cost them the World

Roger Jnr. Roger would have been a good father, according to his widow, Joy. 'Once he'd just arrived home exhausted after training when a bunch of kids knocked on the door asking for his autograph. My grandmother told them it was best to leave him alone for now but he came to the door and signed each one. It seems like he was always good with kids and I imagine he would have been a good dad. We were married six months, and in all I knew him two and a half years. It's not a long time, is it? I don't have millions of memories, but those I do have are very good.'

Cup in Sweden in 1958'. 'Roger was very, very bright,' said former Old Trafford team-mate John Doherty. 'He couldn't tackle, had no left foot – even though he played left full-back – was a poor header of the ball and I have never seen a better left-back in my life. Brains and pace: tackling was demeaning to Roger. He preferred to pinch it or make them give it him. Jimmy Murphy used to say to the full-backs: "Don't tackle them and they will finish up giving you the ball. You have done your job once they cross the ball." Roger was brilliant at that.'

As a member of the 1951/52 title-winning side, Byrne also retained a certain hauteur, with gravitas . . . and occasional intolerance. On one pre-season training camp, he cuffed a youth team player, Wilf McGuinness (later to take over as manager post-Busby) round the ear for daring to take his chair by the hotel pool.

The captain kept his troops in order, particularly the young elements; Eddie Colman in particular. Sandy Busby had a story about Colman falling foul of Roger Byrne the morning after the night before, hours of dancing . . . and a few drinks.

'Sunday morning it was always Mass with Dad and then head off down to the ground. All the lads used to go down, particularly if you were injured. There would be a five-a-side or runs round the ground. This Sunday we had been to a party, the usual gang and we were at the ground at two or three o'clock. Eddie was looking like death.

'Roger was walking down the tunnel when he tells me to leave for a minute. Eddie comes back very red and flustered and Roger had told him he'd better get a grip or he'd be out. It was things like that I thought Roger would be the obvious manager after my dad retired.'

The family club house was in upmarket Urmston where they kept a Morris Minor – 'like hen's teeth in those days', according to Joy – to get to and from work. A boy, later christened Roger, was born in Cottage Hospital, Urmston, 38 weeks after the crash.

NIGHTS ON THE TOWN

As any sportsman will concede you can't spend a whole day on the training pitch and for some of the single players at Old Trafford it became something of a dilemma. The young Bobby Charlton and Liam Whelan killed time with afternoon matinees at one of the many local cinemas and Duncan Edwards would spend hours at Ringway airport, watching planes departing or landing.

Then there were girls.

They were often regarded as an unnecessary evil by many football managers of the 50s and 60s, Busby among them. By the time of Munich, however, most of his players were spoken for.

Then, as now, there was no shortage of admirers.

The rituals of courtship took place in the hundred of cinemas, dance halls and night clubs that enlivened Manchester in the 50s. The city centre had the Gaumont and Odeon cinemas on Oxford Road and the Gaiety on Peter Street where *Gone With the Wind* ran for over a year in front of full houses every night. The Empress in Miles Platting, once the Empress Electric Theatre, was another popular haunt while the Cinephone on Market Street was a slightly more risqué venue, earning a dubious reputation for showing 'foreign' films with titillating titles like *And God Created Woman* or *L'Amore*.

And for the younger, less cerebral, footballers with time on their hands in the afternoon, the masked avenger Zorro and inter-planetary hero Flash Gordon put wrongs to rights in the matinees at the News Theatre on Oxford Road. Learning to dance properly was a social necessity, too.

At the Ritz Ballroom in Whitworth Street aspirant Fred Astaires could hire a professional partner and whirl and twirl in front of a live big band and there were specialist teachers like Tommy Rogers, who ran a studio on Oxford Road.

'You worked your way up,' said Sandy Busby who was on the books of Blackburn Rovers. 'Going to the Plaza was a big scene. That was on Saturday night. Sunday it would be Chorlton and Levenshulme Palais. There was drink because you needed the Dutch courage to go up and ask a girl for a dance and most of the lads were quite shy. David Pegg was always well groomed, very, very smart. Dave, Tommy and Jackie were always big pals; they used to knock around together. They all had similar backgrounds, all working class, but always very polite, which helped with the girls. If you didn't get a girl you'd go to the Ping Hong restaurant on Oxford Street, across from the old Gaumont picture house. The Kardomah (where Dennis Viollet courted his second wife Helen), was popular as were the Espresso Bongo, Denos, the Continental and the Whisky-a-Go-Go.'

Some of the players favoured a members' club called the Cromford in Cromford Court, close by the site of what was then the Arndale Shopping Centre. They had to behave there, though, because Busby used the place, too.

What many of us remember most about Manchester in the 50s . . .the fog! It's 1.30pm in the afternoon on Oxford Street but it may as well be night.

Above: Frankie Vaughan tries out the new craze, The Twist, with 21-year-old Glennys Godderidge during a night out in the Whisky-a-Go-Go in January, 1962. The club (formerly the Rialto cinema on the corner of Bury New Road and Great Cheetham Street, Salford) was quite popular with some players in the 60s.

Above right: Nicholas the Hippo, one of the stars at Belle Vue Zoo, meets a new fan.

'It was a good place to take girlfriends,' said Sandy, 'and as long as they weren't breaking the rules, Dad was quite happy with the lads being there. He'd often send them a drink over. We would go there after the pubs closed to do a little gambling at the tables, watch the floor show, and have a good meal of scampi.'

The club's trendsetter, according to most of the people who knew him (Nobby Stiles idolised him as a youngster), was Eddie Colman. When the Teddyboy craze swept Britain, he bought a jacket with a velvet collar and bumper shoes and forsook Sinatra and Sarah Vaughan for Bill Haley and the early Elvis. Inevitably, he came close to overstepping the mark at times.

Sandy Busby socialised with many of the players (with full knowledge of his dad) and remembered: 'David Pegg and Eddie and myself got home late one night after a party and we were down at Old Trafford next day. The state they were in. David and Eddie were trying to stay out of Dad's way, but Dad had a habit of going in the dressing room and going for a pee and usually while he was there he would ask Tom Curry about any injuries from Saturday. He went in the loo on the left of the big bath and came out a couple of minutes later saying: "Tom, tell Pegg and Colman they can come out of the toilets now." They were unshaven and dying. Dad knew where they had been.'

There was little in the way of scandal. Byrne, Bent, Mark Jones, Jackie Blanchflower, Gregg and Johnny Berry were married, some with children; Liam Whelan and Duncan Edwards were both engaged while Tommy Taylor and Eddie Colman were 'going steady'. Busby did have 'problems' with Viollet, who was married at 17, but carried on like a bachelor after Munich.

There was a spell when Whelan was so homesick he considered returning home but for most there was no incentive to move. Every First Division club at the time were paid the same, the maximum, which ensured that these clubs, and others like Bolton, Preston, Blackpool and Burnley, retained their best players, most of whom were local, too: Finney at Preston, Lofthouse at Bolton, Matthews and Mortensen at Blackpool.

Albert Scanlon, the original Mister Memory, recalled it another way: 'It was an exciting time because we were all children of the war and you could feel the country reviving. The kids seemed to represent that with all that youth and energy. Old Trafford used to be like one happy family. Two ladies we called Omo and Daz used to do the laundry and the lads used to take all their clothes to them. Pre-season, the training was running, jumping, and the only ball we saw was a medicine ball. At training we played married men against single men and it was blood and thunder. Then the fog used to come on to The Cliff off the River Irwell and all

Above left: American folk icon Burl Ives tries out a 1904 De Dion outside the Gaumont Theatre, Oxford Street in July 1953. Burl was on tour and the car was one of the entries in that year's Veteran Car Rally.

Above right: See you later, alligator! Bill Haley, minus his Comets but with his famous kiss curl, takes a break during one of his appearances at Manchester's Odeon cinema. The date was 13 February 1957.

you could see was this white ball. If it got too bad we played silly games, like hide and seek. Tommy Taylor, they could never find him, he was the world champion. No one knew where he was. Someone else once shinned up a flagpole. Another hid under a wheelbarrow. Here I was, little more than a schoolboy, hiding in a training ground lavatory cubicle while some of football's biggest names tried to find me.'

Players got a handwritten letter every Friday with a detailed report on how they had performed the previous time along with a description of the opposition they would face next time: who they would mark and who would be marking them.

Fans still speak in awe of the youth team of 1992 and there's even a Netflix documentary (*The Class of 92*), starring Ryan Giggs, the Neville brothers, David Beckham, Paul Scholes and Nicky Butt. Supporters of an earlier vintage (me) will happily talk of the Class of 52 as their equals, if not their betters: Clayton, Fulton, Kennedy, Colman, Cope, Edwards, McFarlane, Whelan, Doherty, Lewis, Pegg and Scanlon. By the time you get to Edwards there's nothing left to dispute but let me ass: All 12 were 16 or 17 when they played in the first team and all were spotted, nurtured and developed by Jimmy Murphy. It's a remarkable achievement, particularly if contrasted that to the vast resources a Manchester United manager and his assistants have today.

It was an exciting time for all of us. Rationing had ended and there was virtual full employment. We've never had it so good, as someone put it. The first electric iron appeared in our kitchen along with a noisy washing machine (though no telly or motor car yet). Scanlon was right: there was a definitive sense of optimism, the feeling of emerging from a dark tunnel into daylight. Suddenly there were trips to local cinemas (three in little Middleton where I lived), speedway and a zoo at Belle Vue, boxing and wrestling at King's Hall and all sorts of scary stuff at Blackpool Pleasure Beach.

There was skating at the Ice Palace by Cheetham Hill where captain Roger Byrne first courted his wife-to-be and where Bobby Charlton met his Norma. There was cricket

The bulk of the Munich team are pictured early in 1958. Left to right, back row: trainer Tom Curry, Duncan Edwards, Mark Jones, Ray Wood, Bobby Charlton, Bill Foulkes and Busby. Front row: Johnny Berry, Liam Whelan, Roger Byrne, David Pegg and Eddie Colman. 'Our whole little world revolved round Jimmy Murphy, Bert Whalley and Tom,' said Albert Scanlon.

at the southern end of Warwick Road . . . and football at the 'other' Old Trafford.

Middleton wasn't typical Manchester United territory. Many locals I grew up with supported Oldham or Rochdale. A journey to Old Trafford was a major expedition: a ten-minute walk to the main road, a bus to Cannon Street, a train from Central station to the rail halt and a final sprint to the ground. The game that changed my little landscape forever was on Christmas Day, 1955 when I watched goals from Dennis Viollet (2), Roger Byrne, Tommy Taylor and John Doherty in a 5-1 defeat of Charlton.

The memories of Old Trafford then were of swaying masses in the vast, open terraces, Johnny Ray and Jimmy Young on the loud speaker, the Woodbines and Hamlets . . . and the smog. Three years later the smog was still there . . . but most everything else had gone.

Daily Mirror

FRI FEB 7 1958

2½ᴰ FORWARD WITH THE PEOPLE
No. 16,843

SOCCER AIR TRAGEDY

Manchester United plane crashes

22 dead

THE END The chartered Elizabethan airliner in which the Manchester United team was travelling home lies shattered | in a snowfield near Munich. The pilot, Captain James Thain, escaped alive from the smashed nose (on the left of the picture).

CRUNCHIE makes exciting biting! 4ᴰ

THE BEGINNING This picture was taken when the team, accompanied by sports writers, boarded the plane at Manchester on Monday. Left to right, with known survivors marked with asterisk*: Jackie Blanchflower*; Billy Foulkes*; Walter Crickmer, secretary; Don Davies, Man- | chester Guardian; Roger Byrne, captain; Duncan Edwards*; Albert Scanlon*—just visible behind Scanlon is Frank Swift, News of the World; Ray Wood*; Denis Viollet*; Archie Ledbrooke, Daily Mirror; Geoff Bent; Mark Jones and Alf Clarke, Kemsley Newspapers.

AN Elizabethan airliner, on charter to the fabulous Manchester United football team, crashed in flames at Munich Airport, Germany, yesterday, and plunged the world of Soccer into mourning.

Last night twenty-two men—among them some of the brightest stars in British football—were feared to have died in the crash.

Seven of them were members of the champion Manchester United football team—such international stars as Roger Byrne, the team captain, and centre forward Tommy Taylor.

Twenty-two of the forty-four people aboard the plane survived, including Matt Busby, the team's famous manager, two air hostesses and a baby.

Among those who died was Archie Ledbrooke, the Mirror's famous Northern sports writer.

● THE CRASH—Story and pictures: Back Page.
● THE TEAM in the Tragedy—See Centre Pages.

—Blackest Day of—
All—By Peter Wilson
—See Page 23—

● 'There's not a lot left to say after this, is there?' asked my dad, showing me the front page of the *Daily Mirror*. Dad had served with the paras during the war and was quite cynical about death and how it was reported. The day after the disaster, 7 February, it was all there: images of the wrecked plane, numbers of dead, names of the dead, names of the living, quotes from a survivor, who happened to be a *Daily Mail* photographer. On the same day armies of

reporters, photographers and camera crews flew out to Munich while others chased down grieving families at home. There was no question of waiting until 'the next of kin have been informed' back then. Inside Munich's Rechts der Isar Hospital and at the crash site journalists and photographers wandered at will, even catching images of Busby (who had been given the last rites) in an oxygen tent and Edwards on what was to be his deathbed.

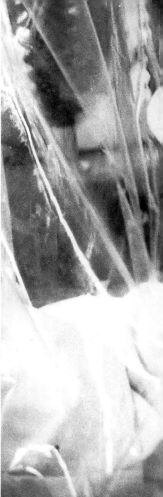

The *Mirror* and the *Express*, the biggest selling UK newspapers at the time (the *Express* employed over 200 staff writers and photographers) called in what Walter Winchell used to call the '400-pound gorillas', the imperious columnists of the day: Peter Wilson, The Man You Can't Gag of the *Mirror*, Des Hackett, The Man in the Brown Bowler, of the *Express*.

All of this hit the streets within some 12 hours of the disaster, in some cases breaking the news to bereaved families. Like us, many didn't have a TV or radio or telephone.

'The doorbell rang at 7am on the day after and it was a policeman,' said Irene Beevers, the sister of David Pegg. 'He didn't waste words and said straight out: "Tha'

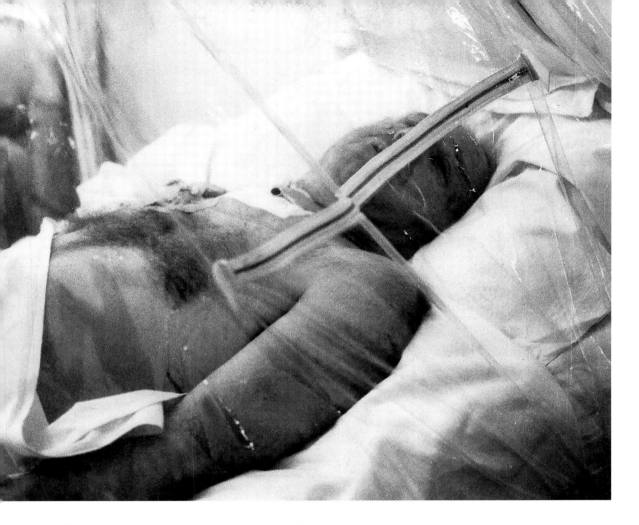

David's dead, what dost want doing with t'body?" I will never forget this big man in uniform stood there in the door. He just walked straight in and came out with that and it's exactly what he said. There's no nice way of saying it I know, but there's nicer ways of saying it.'

Others were more sensitive with some of the news informed by Busby's assistant Jimmy Murphy, seated in his office in the dark, empty stadium, phone in front of him and a bottle of whisky alongside.

'"From all that's left at Old Trafford" – that's how he said it,' Christy, brother of Liam Whelan, says in his home at Portmarnock, Co. Dublin – "from all that's left at Old Trafford – we wish you all condolences and will be in touch".'

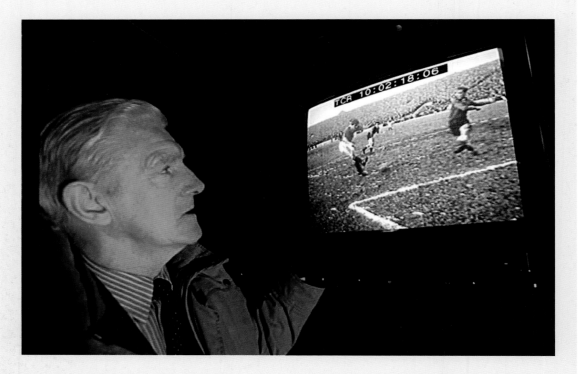

● Bill Foulkes watches the 5 February 1958 coverage of Dennis Viollet's goals against Red Star in Belgrade where the 3–3 draw won a place in the European Cup semi-final. The film had been enhanced in colour for a TV documentary, *The Busby Babes: The End of a Dream.*

It wasn't until his death in 2013 that Bill's true worth to his club and as a man became clear. Unlike many, for example, he never milked the disaster and seldom, in public at least, spoke about it.

Some claimed, incorrectly, that his long career at Old Trafford owed everything to the deaths of better players at Munich to which the obvious response is to point out that Foulkes was in the starting line-up in Belgrade.

Unlike the luckless Geoff Best he was certainly not there as cover. There were some accusations of cowardice after the crash, notably from Harry Gregg, who was once quoted as saying: 'You should have seen the big fucker run. ' In fact, Foulkes had been obeying orders from the captain, James Thain, (ignored by Gregg to his eternal credit) to get as far away as quickly as possible because 'she was going to blow'.

Foulkes was too taciturn and unemotional for many fans and football writers (one accused him of 'doing an Alf [Ramsey] and having elocution lessons because he 'doesn't sound like a Lancashire collier'. In fact Foulkes came from a proud family sporting tradition. Both grandfather and father had played rugby league for St Helens and Bill's bulk and aggression could have followed them. Instead he signed for Manchester United in 1951, while keeping his job at Lea Green Colliery. Pay was better at the pit and the maximum wage still applied to professional footballers.

He made his debut in a 2–1 win at Anfield on 13 December 1952, the first of a then record 688 games for the club. He earned one cap for England, playing alongside Billy Wright at full-back, in a 2–0 win over Northern Ireland on 2 October 1954.

After Manchester United's victory at Wembley in 1968 he wrote: 'What I do know is that ten years afterwards, I still think about those who went and I wonder why I escaped unhurt.' He never once discussed it with Busby. His medals and other mementoes were auctioned at Christie's in October 1992.

The men who made Manchester United . . . Knight of the Realm Sir Matt Busby and plain Jimmy Murphy, the de facto manager in 1958 when Busby was fighting for his life in a Munich hospital. Murphy's worth and commitment to United were immeasurable. As Sir Bobby Charlton said: 'I learnt a lot from Matt Busby and Alf Ramsey but everything I achieved in football I owe to one man and one man only: Jimmy Murphy. Matt and Alf were good to me, but Jimmy got to my guts. Jimmy was simply sensational.' Munich survivor Harry Gregg agreed: 'He was the making of Charlton. He got him to cut out the glory balls early on and bollocked him for attempting the difficult when something simpler was more productive. The work he did with the kids was phenomenal.'

MURPHY'S

There is an excellent biography by Wayne Barton, published at the same time as the 60th anniversary of Munich, that demonstrates what we have long believed: that whether deliberately or not, the worth of Jimmy Murphy to the club was badly underestimated.

Barton wrote: 'I could pay Jimmy no higher compliment than describing him as the most important man in United's history. Without him, there probably

LAW

wouldn't have been a club, but even if there was, it would be far different. The reality is he had much more to do with the creation of the Busby Babes than many acknowledge.'

If asked to rate the most significant men in the history of Old Trafford I would always put Murphy first, Busby second, James Gibson – the man who hired Busby and whose finances kept the club alive – third. Alex Ferguson would be somewhere after that.

Busby and Murphy had played against each other at club level in the 30s; Murphy as a wing-half for Swindon (and a holder of 15 Welsh caps) and Busby for Manchester City and Liverpool, among others. As they say in journalism, when the truth becomes legend always print the legend so the approved story now is that they first met at a transit camp in Bari, Italy towards the end of the war. Busby had heard one of Murphy's rabble-rousing team talks to a group of football-playing soldiers and had determined to sign him.

Like most flourishing double acts they had little in common apart from upbringings in straitened circumstances, strict Catholic upbringings, a fondness for Scotch whisky . . . and football. Murphy excelled on the training ground and Busby in the manager's office (his injuries at Munich limited his activity).

Jimmy Murphy and his glory boys from the World Cup of '58 were still hard at it ahead of the British Home Championship match against England in November, 1963: John Charles is on the right with Ivor Allchurch (left) and Roy Vernon with his back to the camera. Unfortunately, Wales lost all three games and Jimmy's tenure ended after the 2–1 defeat by Scotland at Hampden Park (one of the goals coming from Denis Law).

After 6 February 1958 and for some time afterwards Murphy had to go it alone and he rose to the challenge. While tending the families of the Munich dead and the survivors he guided a rag-tag outfit of youngsters from the reserves and bought-in veterans (notably Ernie Taylor of Blackpool and England and Stan Crowther of Aston Villa) to the FA Cup Final. Crucially, he also persuaded Munich survivor Bill Foulkes to take over the captaincy, much against his will. The fact the Nat Lofthouse and Bolton won that final 2–0 was irrelevant, Michael Parkinson, a

● Dressed to kill . . . Bert Whalley and Murphy get ready for action. Like the pre-Munich Busby, Murphy always went to work in a baggy tracksuit tucked into a pair of woollen socks. Whalley, a former wing-half at Old Trafford, joined the coaching team in 1947 and was third in command after Busby and Murphy. He took his job very seriously and some of his coaching ideas are mirrored today. Before a match a handwritten letter was delivered to every player with a detailed opinion on how they had played the week before, along with a description of the team and players of the opposition they would face the following week.

Like trainer Tom Curry and his deputy Bill Inglis, Whalley always wore a white coat to work, resembling rather jolly cricket umpires. While Murphy snapped and snarled, they smiled and cajoled. 'Our whole little world revolved round Jimmy Murphy, Bert Whalley and Tom Curry,' said Albert Scanlon. 'The staff made it so happy, people like the laundry ladies. The older players were more reserved but they would still join in the fun. You had respect for the first-teamers, but the kids were in a little world of our own.'

Whalley, who had been invited on the last trip as a bonus, and Curry were to die at Munich. It was fortunate for United that Murphy wasn't aboard, having taken over as part-time coach to Wales who were soon to take part in the World Cup in Sweden.

Light training will do ahead of the trip to Sheffield Wednesday on 29 March 1958. Jimmy Murphy and Bill Inglis watch as Stan Crowther, Freddie Goodwin, Shay Brennan, Alex Dawson and Bobby Harrop show their paces. Some interesting characters there: Alex Dawson, the Black Prince as he was known, should never have left Old Trafford judging by his scoring record (54 goals in 93 games, including a hat-trick in the 1958 semi-final against Fulham). He was also a mean cricketer. He regularly turned out as an all-rounder for Fulwood and Broughton in the Northern League and even scored a match-winning 32 not out in one match in May 1964. He was no Fred Trueman (though the resemblance was remarkable) but definitely better than your average footballer!

far better writer than a chat show host in my opinion, got it right when he insisted that Murphy and the United team that reached Wembley (86 days after Munich), were never accorded the recognition they deserved. Murphy, almost single-handedly, had also showed there was still life at Old Trafford.

Harry Gregg (bundled over the line by Lofthouse for the second goal in an uncanny rerun of the 1957 defeat by Aston Villa) said: 'Jimmy would take broken-hearted players and spin them a fairy story. He'd cry with you, sing with you, a lovable, outlandish, crazy Welshman with an Irish name.'

Gregg also witnessed the man's essential humanity: 'I remember in the hotel after the crash watching a flake at a time come down and the families arrive. I got sick of going up and down in the hospital lift so I decided to walk up the stairs which were not well lit. Before I got to top flight I could hear this terrible sobbing from round the corner. I looked round and Jimmy Murphy was sat halfway up the top flight crying his eyes out. I just turned and went back down.'

Murphy's feats in Sweden were remarkable; particularly the Wales defeat of Hungary in a play-off after both

A couple of strangers infiltrate the squad on 8 July 1964, the day United reported back for training. England cricketer Geoff Boycott is on the left, with his chairman of selectors, Walter Robins, 6th from the left just before the fourth Test against Australia at Old Trafford. Others in the line-up are left to right: John Aston snr, Wilf McGuiness, Graham Moore, Jimmy Murphy, Jimmy Nicholson, David Sadler, Jimmy Ryan, Alan Duff, Albert Kinsey, Ed Harrop, Denis Law, Wilf Tranter, Maurice Setters, Mike Lorimer, Tony Mallalieu, Tony Dunne, David Gaskell, David Herd, Albert Quixall, Pat Dunne, Shay Brennan, Nobby Stiles, John Connelly, George Best, Pat Crerand, Noel Cantwell, Harry Gregg, Matt Busby. Kneeling: Barry Grayson, Eamonn Dunphy (yes, that one), Bobby Noble, Bobby Smith, Bill Anderson, Ken Morton, John Fitzpatrick, Bernard Marshall, Peter McBride, Glendon Andrews and Ted Dalton.

countries had finished level on points. These were not the Magnificent Magyars of the early 50s (no Ferenc Puskás who left Hungary after the 1956 revolution) but they could still boast József Bozsik and captain Nandor Hidegkuti. Wales finally lost 1–0 to eventual champions Brazil, but Murphy was suddenly manager of the month. Arsenal tried to sign him, as did Juventus and, after the World Cup, Brazil. He turned them all down; maybe he was more interested in getting Puskás to Old Trafford!

It would be nice to believe that this remarkable man's dedication to Manchester United was reciprocated, but sadly it wasn't. After Busby retired, Murphy was given the title of club scout, and then side-lined by a succession of managers who plainly saw him as an anachronism.

Bobby Charlton is cornered by Busby and Eamonn Andrews with his *This Is Your Life* album.

> **Busby sat next to him throughout and the effect was of a prisoner allowed out for the day and a head warder making sure he behaved**

Eventually, he lost his office and United informed him they would no longer pay for his taxis and phone bills.

'By the time Jimmy died in 1989 he and Matt were strangers,' said Gregg. 'It was heart-breaking. Jimmy never showed his feelings but it must have come close to breaking him.'

THERE WAS more proof of the chasm between the two men in November, 1969. Charlton had been invited to take part in 'Great Moment of Sport' at the Sportsman Club and at the end Eamonn Andrews turned up with his This is Your Life album. It was one of the most cringe-making editions ever. Charlton was nervous, monosyllabic and still unsure of himself in public (when wife Norma arrived he shook her hand).

For some reason Busby sat next to him throughout (closer than mum Sissie and dad Bob) and the effect was of a prisoner allowed out for the day and a head warder making sure he behaved. Worst of all, there was not a mention of Jimmy Murphy, the man Charlton has always insisted was the most influential in his career. At the end, just before the credits rolled and Andrews handed over the big red book, Murphy was allowed to walk in with members of the squad at the time. I can remember Andrews' words now: 'And here they are . . . Shay Brennan, Alex Stepney, Tony Dunn, Bill Foulkes, Pat Crerand, David Sadler, Brian Kidd and Johnny Aston . . . and your two good friends assistant manager Jimmy Murphy who like Sir Matt helped so much to shape his career and schoolboy international team-mate and now United manager Wilf McGuinness.' This was an obvious attempt to have the man who had been the sheet-anchor for Busby, his players and the club as a whole erased from the Manchester United history books. It failed.

Heavy snow at Ringway airport as Murphy and Busby lead their Manchester United squad aboard a flight to Dublin. It was 1 February 1963, and the height of the Big Freeze when football schedules had been decimated by one of the coldest winters on record. Desperate to keep his players active Busby fixed up a hastily arranged friendly with Jimmy Hill's Coventry City after it was plain that the weather was not as bad in Ireland. Busby, left, and Murphy, second right, manages a smile though some (Harry Gregg top left, Bobby Charlton two below him and Dennis Viollet midway between Busby and Murphy) look less than happy. Among other players visible here are Nobby Stiles, Johnny Giles, and Albert Quixall.

THERE'S NEVER much in the way of spontaneity at Old Trafford, apart from ideas for new ways of making money. It's invariably the determination and sheer bloody minded-ness of fans that gets things done, like the bust of Murphy in the museum and the media centre that's named after him. Some you win; some you lose.

There were several attempts to get the club to rename the K-Stand after Murphy. The club has always refused to discuss or even responded to such suggestions, though a spokesman did tell the *Mirror*: 'Jimmy Murphy holds a unique and special place in Manchester United's history, which we recognised through the naming of the Jimmy Murphy Centre at the Aon Training Complex [Carrington to us] as a tribute to him in 2012. Whilst we have no imme-diate plans to extend the range of statues at Old Trafford, we are hugely respectful of the immense contribution he has made to the club.'

Another plea from fans and another response from the club 12 months later: 'We can't be building statues for everybody.'

THE LOST BABES

Matt Busby, as he did with George Best later, tended to tolerate flair and the occasional genius in any player. His son Sandy, who socialised with most of the young players (though never snitching to Dad) told me in 2003: 'I remember David Pegg and **EDDIE COLMAN** and myself got home late one night. David and Eddie were trying to stay out of Dad's way, but Dad had a habit of going in the dressing room and going for a pee and usually while he was there he would ask Tom Curry about any injuries from Saturday. He went in the loo on the left of the big bath and came out a couple of minutes later saying: 'Tom, tell Pegg and Colman they can come out of the toilets now.' They were unshaven and dying. Dad knew where they'd been.'

Eddie Colman, an only child, was brought up by his

parents, Dick and Liz, at No 9 Archie Street – the replica of Coronation Street it's said – close by Ordsall Park in Salford. He was nine years old when Germany surrendered and the dark days were over.

He was educated at Ordsall Council School, the same school of Allan Clarke and Graham Nash of The Hollies, where Nash, pre his superstar days, is still remembered in Ordsall for his performance in the school play as an Ugly Sister in *Cinderella*.

Eddie was to become one of the most dazzling and beguiling of the Busby Babes, a boy adored by all and in particular the club king-maker, Jimmy Murphy. Murphy adored little Eddie.

The body swerve earned him the nickname of Snake-hips and he teased the opposition with the drag-back, the push and run into space and the startling speed off the mark. Harry Gregg, who joined the club from Doncaster Rovers in December 1957, called him 'a wee wag with a beer belly'.

'The first time I played with Eddie and even now it's hard to believe this happened,' said Gregg. 'I was in goal and Eddie at wing-half and I was a wanderer. If the ball went forward 20 yards I went forwards 20 yards; if it came back 20 I came back 20. Eddie got the ball and does this wiggle and I found myself doing the same thing!'

As part of three winning FA Youth Cup sides, one of them as captain, Colman's skills had already become part of pub and terrace folklore. Even during his National Service in the mid-50s (Eddie served in the Royal Signals at Catterick) where the Army could field a team of international class – and usually did.

The late Jimmy Armfield, still the uncrowned king of Blackpool, did his National Service in 1954–56 based at Lancaster, and later Aldershot. He played in a British Army team that included Bill Foulkes, Colman and Duncan Edwards.

He said: 'To be honest, I can't remember us ever losing

and we had a fixture list that included Glasgow Rangers and Everton and we even beat Northern Ireland. Eddie was a push and run player, he would shuffle and then go into space. He was a very buoyant character as well and I can remember him getting up at the front of the team bus in Germany to lead a sing-song.'

Forty years after Munich the time came to divide the funds from the Old Trafford memorial match. Eddie, it was then discovered, had no close dependants so his £20k went to charity, the Royal Manchester Children's Research Fund and the NACRO Community Link. Some of the survivors, who were not consulted, believed that Colman's share should have gone 'back in the kitty'. Many were enraged to discover that a large proportion of the gate receipts went to Eric Cantona.

So all that's left now are our memories of Eddie Colman and a few of his items left in the Old Trafford museum. The museum, whose entrance is next to the Red Cafe in the North Stand should anyone wish to see it, is spread over three floors and has a separate room dedicated to Munich. Some may see exhibits that include the passport of Eddie Colman, his provisional driving licence and a letter from the secretary Les Olive to a fan informing him that 'a specialist had informed Johnny Berry that he will unfortunately never play again' in dubious taste, ghoulish even, but there's little doubt it has a fine sense of theatre. Tragedy is always saleable.

Albert Scanlon's passport is open to show a stamp issued by the customs at Belgrade airport, close by Duncan Edwards' poignant telegram to his landlady informing her that the plane had been delayed.

A recording of the original BBC radio broadcast giving news of the crash is played constantly in the background for the benefit of visitors and there are cuttings from newspapers of the time. MATT 50-50: EDWARDS 'GRAVE': BERRY COMA', says one duplicate front page from the *Manchester Evening News*.

> **All that's left now are our memories of Eddie Colman and a few of his items left in the Old Trafford museum**

THIS IS THE most famous picture of **GEOFF BENT**, going man-to-man with Preston North End and England legend Tom Finney in January 1950. Photographers seldom bother with details from captions so this leaves a bit of a mystery: Preston were in the Second Division at the time and the sparsity of the crowd suggests that Geoff (and Finney

The favourite family snap for Marion Bent, her daughter Karen and Karen's young son has to be the newspaper cutting of Geoff taking on Preston and England legend Tom Finney.

who had been injured for a large part of the previous season) were playing for the respective reserve sides. Bent helped the United A team win the Manchester League in the 50/51 season. He had been an apprentice joiner after school (Finney being more famous as the Preston Plumber) and a number of clubs had been keen on signing him. Clara, his mother, had her mind set on Old Trafford and he signed as an amateur in 1949. He signed professional in 1952.

Like one of the cast members in *The Magnificent Seven* Geoff Bent is the name you remember last. A Salford-ian, like Eddie Colman and an only child too, he was born and raised in similar circumstances in Irlams o ' th' Height in September 1932. Dad Cliff, a miner, was a big Swinton rugby league fan though mum Clara was the real driving force.

His early performances as a member of the Barton Villa side in the Eccles & District League earned him a place in the Salford Schoolboys as captain, leading the team to success in the English Schools Shield in 1947. Ironically, the final was held at a packed Old Trafford, its first game played there since the war and the trophy was presented by

England full-back Frank Swift who was also to die at Munich. Bent was 25 (a relative senior in 'Babe' terms) by the time of the crash and had already suffered two broken legs in a career that never really caught fire.

He was understudy at left-back to Byrne, which was never going to offer him many opportunities. Tall, well-built and a strong tackler, it was felt he would eventually take over from John Aston Snr at left-back, until Byrne made his switch from wing to No.3.

Most of his Old Trafford career was spent in the reserves often alongside seven or eight internationals and, half-heartedly, he had twice asked Busby for a move, only to be told he was too valuable. The arrival of his daughter, Karen, late in 1957 and the offer of a club house on King's Road finally settled him.

He shouldn't have gone to Belgrade. Like Byrne he was a notoriously bad flier, usually suffering from nose bleeds, and quite happy to hear that he would be staying at home with his wife Marion and five-month-old Karen when the team sheet was pinned up in the first-team dressing room at Old Trafford.

Byrne suffered a slight strain in the final Arsenal match at Highbury and, as the skipper's stand-by, Geoff would be going to Belgrade after all. In the event, Byrne was fit to face Red Star and Bent flew out as a passenger.

Left with a baby daughter to bring up and with little in the way of recompense for the next four decades, Marion wasn't the type to broadcast her woes to the world. Harry

Geoff Bent training at Old Trafford in March 1957, a few days after winning one of his 12 first-team appearances (a 2–1 win at Everton).

Gregg said: 'I was at the post-match function at Bolton on the 40th anniversary and I saw Marion standing outside with her daughter. She told me she didn't feel she had the right to be there. Hadn't the right! I took her inside and sat her down with some of the other wives she had been close to when Geoff was alive.'

THERE'S A FAMOUS Monty Python sketch in which four Yorkshiremen sit and drink and brag about their humble upbringing and try to prove they grew up more deprived than everyone else. The sketch has always reminded me of the pub conversations I had with Manchester United fans of my era (and still occasionally do) and which usually go like this: 'I was born in the same street as Dennis' or 'I went to school with Roger's lad' or 'I once saw **LIAM WHELAN** in the News Theatre on Oxford Road.' The last one is my own and true and though I always feel foolish offering this as a Busby Babes anecdote, it's all part of being a fan and my own attempt to be associated in some way with a team and a particular player.

I also used to wonder what a footballer, and a well-known one at that, was doing, alone and in a near empty cinema watching an afternoon matinee (though he wouldd probably also wonder what a 12-year-old schoolboy was doing there). Some 45 years later when I met Liam Whelan's brother, Christy, at his home in Portmarnock, Co. Dublin it was all explained.

'One of the problems Liam had was how he spent the days,' Christy said. 'He would train all morning and finish about 1pm and go to pictures in town. The afternoons were a terrible drag.'

He was homesick a lot of the time, too. 'In Manchester

Liam Whelan gives Charlton a lift on the way to Sir Bobby's hat-trick in the 5–1 win at Charlton on 19 February 1957. Two goals came from Tommy Taylor with a rare appearance in the first team for Geoff Bent at full-back. The Addicks keeper is Willie Duff, fresh from National Service and a worthy replacement for the legendary Sam Bartram.

he never really settled down. "I wish it was all over so I could come home and open a business," he would say. But he did find a home there. Sean Dolan, who worked for Louis Edwards, who later became the Manchester United chairman, lived on the edge of Stockport and Liam was there one day playing with the two children when all of a sudden Brenda, Sean's wife says: "Would you like to stay here?" So he moved there and if he had happiness in Manchester this was it, this was his home from home.'

Liam's father, John Whelan Snr, died in 1942, 11 years before his son signed for Manchester United and there were two brothers, John and Christy and sisters Rita, Maura and Alice.

Christy said: 'Daddy worked for the corporation, and contracted TB. Mammy was left with all the children and we never wanted for anything. None of us were working and although we didn't have everything, we never wanted.'

Liam's first club was Home Farm that at various times

A relaxed first-team squad a day before the FA Cup quarter-final meeting with Bournemouth and Boscombe Athletic at Dean Court (aka Fitness First Stadium, Seward Stadium, Goldsands Stadium and Vitality Stadium) in March, 1957. United won 2–1 in the end against a Third Division (South) team that had seen off Wolves and Spurs on the way. Maybe Duncan Edwards, Johnny Berry, Dennis Viollet, Bill Foulkes, Roger Byrne, Wilf McGuinness, Mark Jones and Liam Whelan should have taken them more seriously!

Liam went just wide with this attempt but finished up with a double in the 4–0 defeat of Sunderland in front of 58,726 fans at Old Trafford. Duncan Edwards and Tommy Taylor were other goal-scorers. Sunderland could boast a host of class players, including North East legend Stan Anderson, Northern Ireland's Billy Bingham, ageing 'Clown Prince' Len Shackleton and one Don Revie on the wing. The Wearsiders were to finish third from bottom of the First Division.

has boasted the great Johnny Carey (much later seen by Harry Gregg reading electricity meters in Sale), Liam and another great Whelan, the former Liverpool player Ronnie. The United and Leeds player John Giles and the Leeds full-back Gary Kelly, along with some 50 senior Republic of Ireland internationals, also began their careers there.

Christy remembers: 'Liam went to United in 1953 and he would come home for the internationals. The local kids would knock on the door: "Is Liam coming out to play?" He'd go out in the street to play and come back later and say: "Well, a hat-trick at Dalymount and a hat-trick on the road, what do you think of that?" He was always very humble and very down to earth.'

He played only four games for his country, but one of them the memorable 1–1 draw against England at Dalymount Park in May 1957 playing alongside future United captain Noel Cantwell. Later asked who he rated as the greatest English player of all time, Cantwell said: 'I never played with Duncan Edwards, but I played against

him in perhaps the most famous World Cup game ever staged in Dublin and Liam Whelan nutmegged Duncan twice. I don't think Duncan was best pleased.'

On the field it had become almost easy for Liam and Manchester United. In 1955/56 they had mopped up the championship with two games to spare and 11 points clear. The following season they carried on where they had left off. True, they were being beaten home and away by local nemesis Bolton but the firepower Busby and Jimmy Murphy could muster was almost frightening. Most think of Tommy Taylor, Bobby Charlton and Dennis Viollet, but the marksman of the season was Liam Whelan, with 26 goals out of a team total of 103.

Irish football fans, of a certain vintage at least, have no hesitation in placing Liam alongside Peter Doherty, John Giles and Liam Brady in the hall of fame of great home-bred midfielders. Looking at his record and his 96 all-competition appearances for Manchester United he hit the target 52 times a phenomenal strike rate for an inside- forward . . . and this was the start of his career.

Another carefree posed picture taken at the Midland Hotel in Manchester after the 2–0 FA Cup semi-final win over Birmingham at Hillsborough in March 1957. The partiers are, left to right: (teetotaller!) Liam Whelan, Wilf McGuinness (who didn't play), saxophonist Tommy Taylor, David Pegg and Bobby Charlton who scored one of the goals. Johnny Berry got the other.

As John Whelan, a fine footballer in his own right for Drumcondra, pointed out to me: 'Ruud van Nistelrooy equalled Liam's record of eight consecutive goals for United in 2002/03, but Liam was never given any penalties to take in 56/57!'

Christy added: 'Bobby Charlton wanted to be the best player in the world but didn't think he would be while Liam was around.'

It was always believed that Liam would have joined the priesthood when his football career was over, but in fact he had a girlfriend in Dublin, Ruby McCullagh, and they were due to marry in June 1958. Ruby was 20 and they had known other for two or three years, according to Rita Whelan, who was still living in the family home in Cabra, on Dublin's northside when I met her in 2004.

'At the cup final of 1957, I was with Ruby when the game was over and Jean Blanchflower's wife began to cry; she felt that Jackie having to go in goal had cost them the game. Liam cried as well. I can close my eyes now and still see him waving at me and Mammy from the Wembley pitch.'

Liam had asked to be left out of the ill-fated Belgrade trip. He had just lost his place to Charlton, was suffering with a heavy cold and as his mother had been poorly, too, he felt he could benefit from a rest in Dublin. Busby decided 'it wouldn't look right' if Whelan didn't travel with the squad. His family were never to question the perversities of fate or, like some of the survivors, seek recrimination.

'We accepted that he had gone to Heaven and that God had wanted him,' said Rita. 'We never asked why. We never went into things like that. Liam died on the Thursday and the following morning, the first Friday, was Communion and Mammy had us round Christ the King Church in Cabra. It was our faith brought us through it. Nor have we ever asked anything of United. All the money in the world couldn't bring Liam back to us.'

> **Bobby Charlton wanted to be the best player in the world but didn't think he would be while Liam was around**

● David Pegg, dapper and stylish as ever, follows the rather less dapper and stylish Bobby Charlton down Preston station platform on the way to Wembley. Ahead is the FA Cup Final heartbreak against Aston Villa and 2–1 defeat.

Charlton and Pegg were best friends at Old Trafford. Charlton idolised the young Yorkshireman who had taken the shy Ashington lad under his wing when he first arrived from the North East. It was an unlikely friendship. Pegg had film star looks and a ready smile, Charlton unprepossessing. After

Pegg bought his first car, a light–blue Vauxhall Victor, Charlton did likewise. His was dark blue and Tommy Taylor followed suit with a red one and the three of them – in three separate cars – would motor in convoy across to the West Riding home of Pegg's parents in Highfields, arriving much to the astonishment of the locals.

'Our David took Bob under his wing,' said Pegg's sister, Irene. 'Bob was shy but a smashing lad. I think he had problems with George Best later because of the examples of David, Liam Whelan and the others.'

'I want the boy to be happy Mr Busby, but if it doesn't go well for him it's back to the pits. Will he make the grade?'

CANNY BOSS Matt Busby always made sure everything was done by the book. On **DAVID PEGG**'s 17th birthday, the day he was old enough to turn professional, his father was invited to Old Trafford. Bill Pegg, a miner for 48 years and a man determined his son would never do the same, told Busby: 'I want the boy to be happy Mr Busby, but if it doesn't go well for him it's back to the pits. Will he make the grade?'

'As long as he keeps trying,' said Busby. 'That's all I ask of any lad.' He always asked for a bit more (the guess is he didn't tell Bill Pegg of this) because Busby was scolding the 17-year-old Tyke within days of his arrival at Old Trafford.

'It's never too early or too late to wear a tie,' Busby told Pegg, caught wearing an open-necked shirt. Pegg smiled back and agreed.

'You see all those pictures of our David, always with a smile on his face?' his sister Irene Beevers asked of me. 'That was exactly how he was. He was just a genuinely nice lad. We were miners' kids and lived in a mining village and we were just ordinary kids and there's no doubt David was the light of our dad's eye.'

He was 15 when he left Highfields school (infant, juniors and seniors sharing shared the same quadrangle) and he needed dispensation to leave early. It was agreed he should serve as an apprenticeship joiner, but in the end football took over.

'Most weeks he came home with his shirts for ironing,' said Irene. '"No one can iron shirts like my mum," he would say. There's a famous picture of David in his digs at Mrs Watson's doing the dishes. He didn't do dishes; he didn't do anything about the house. I think he told the photographer: "I'll hold the cloth but I'm not using it."'

He took his responsibilities as a Manchester United footballer seriously, however. As did Tommy Taylor, whose family found a guide to public-speaking in his Manchester digs when they eventually went to collect his belongings.

'David would often be invited back to school to present cups and to local galas to give speeches and he rehearsed all the speeches and learned how to speak in public. Tommy did the same. David also practised signing autographs. David had a lot of girlfriends, but he was not a committer. He was very good-looking and I had loads of friends who were after him. I sang in a girls' choir, the Wheatsheaf Girls' Choir, and lots of lasses would ask if David was coming.

'Sean, my son, is like our David; a smiler. When Mum was in a home she used to look at him and he smiled and I think she sees our David.'

Like every other family, the Peggs were traumatised by Munich, the effects hardly helped by the manner in which they heard the news.

'When we found out we didn't know where he was, we didn't even know he was abroad,' said Irene. 'The doorbell rang at 7am on the day after the crash and it was a policeman. He didn't waste words and said straight out: "Tha' David's dead, what dost want doing with t'body?" I will never forget this big man in uniform stood there in the door. He just walked straight in and came out with that and it's exactly what he said. There's no nice way of saying it I know, but there's nicer ways of saying it.

'That was Friday morning and then all hell broke loose. Mother had the worst time, she was devastated. Dad was strong. "We won't have any of this blubbering" he said on the day of the funeral. Everyone had to have a stiff upper lip. I thought for a while my mother was going to go mental. There was thousands at the funeral, and all these people in the house that no one knew. Policemen were directing traffic, the road was closed and that's what did Mum in. It was as if the Queen was coming. It were awful. You're there just as a bystander, but he was my brother, not an international footballer.'

Pegg, who was 22, didn't leave much in the way of worldly goods.

'Dad and Uncle Frank went to Mrs Watson's in Manchester to fetch his car. Our Sean has his Real Madrid watch and tie. I go to the cemetery every two weeks and on special

> "
> **Someone still puts a flower on his grave. I know which flowers I put on and there is still someone leaves a flower on it**

occasions make sure it's all cleaned up. As for Manchester United, I knew the old school and they are not there anymore. A couple of times I've rung and asked for tickets for my grandson. Someone still puts a flower on his grave. I know which flowers I put on and there is still someone leaves a flower on it. I'd love to know who it is. The grave is in good order and some folk think the club look after it; lots who believe they pay for the flowers on the grave. Maybe it's because they're red and white.'

IT WAS A REMARKABLE display of comradeship from both winners and losers (though not as rare as one would think in those days). With the job done and a place in the European Cup semi-final secured United officials and players joined their Red Star Belgrade opposite numbers at the official banquet in the Majestic Hotel in Belgrade where Roger Byrne led the singing of 'We'll Meet Again' and the White Rose trio of Mark Jones, **TOMMY TAYLOR** and David Pegg offered their rendition of 'On Ilkley Moor Baht 'At'.

In The Crystal nightclub later Taylor and his new pal Dragoslav Sekuralac drunkenly embraced and vowed to stay in touch. Taylor would one day return to Belgrade and the multitalented Slav striker promised he would visit Barnsley. Later, Sekuralac, who died in January 2019, was to break down and weep when he realised it would never happen.

Tommy Taylor was born in Smithies, near Barnsley in 1932, one of six children and, like many youngsters in Barnsley seemingly bound for the pits. He was 16 and playing for his local collier team when Barnsley snapped him up in July 1949. After 28 goals in 46 games for Barnsley and the team's inability to get out of the Second Division the big boys moved in.

Taylor had signalled his arrival at Old Trafford with a scoring header (from outside the penalty area) against Preston on 7 March 1953 and from then on managed

> **It was said he could head a ball more accurately than many players could kick it. This spectacular talent tended to obscure his other abilities**

● Tommy Taylor scores the first goal in the friendly against Brazil at Wembley in May 1956.

It was a dramatic night. Supervet Stanley Matthews had been recalled by England and the Brazilians threatened to walk off at one stage when the referee awarded a penalty against them.

Bristol City striker John Atyeo failed with the kick, as did Roger Byrne later. Unlike the FA who didn't like the notion of rule changes (the main reason Manchester United lost the 1957 FA Cup Final at Wembley) FIFA allowed substitutes for any injured player (before the 44th minute) and a goalkeeper (at any time). United goalkeeper Ray Wood was on the bench (as was Johnny Berry) to cover for Reg Matthews.

The England squad (minus Tom Finney) photographed at Chelsea ahead of the international against Spain at Wembley on 30 November 1955. Back row: Ronnie Clayton, Jeff Hall, Billy Wright, Ron Baynham, Reg Matthews, Jimmy Dickinson and Roger Byrne. Front row: Nat Lofthouse, John Atyeo, Bedford Jezzard, Tommy Taylor, Duncan Edwards, Johnny Haynes and Bill Perry. England won 4–1, with goals from Perry (2), Atyeo and Finney. Duncan and Tommy spent the evening on the subs' bench.

two goals every three matches, with 16 in 19 games for England. It made Tommy Taylor an instant hero for a club desperate for a traditional centre-forward (and England just as desperate for a replacement for the 30-something Nat Lofthouse).

He wasn't a 'Busby Babe' in the official sense of the word (not home-grown, unlike his fellow Tykes Mark Jones and David Pegg) as Busby had broken the transfer record by paying Barnsley £29,999.

Busby, so it's said, hadn't wanted him burdened with a £30,000 price tag, but newspapers being newspapers Taylor was immediately labelled The First £30k Footballer.

It was said he could head a ball more accurately than many players could kick it. This spectacular talent tended to obscure his other abilities. He could look clumsy on the ball but he possessed fine control and astute distribution. His partnership with Dennis Viollet was devastatingly productive.

His fame soon spread and immediately after the

Royden Wood hangs on to this one from Taylor, but there was little else the Leeds goalkeeper could do in a 5-0 win for Manchester United on 7 September 1957. There were doubles for Tommy and Johnny Berry and one from Dennis Viollet. Wood retired (at the age of 29) two years later, managed a betting shop and became one of the leading lights in the PFA and helping to force the Football League and clubs to abolish the £20 a week maximum wage.

Tommy, a keen snooker player, during an R&R session at Davyhulme Park Golf Club ahead of the home game against Bolton on 22 January 1955; Bill Foulkes is awaiting his turn in the background. Tommy scored in a 1–1 draw, with the Bolton equaliser coming from Dennis Stevens, who not only came from Dudley, but was a cousin of Duncan Edwards.

1957 FA Cup Final, in which he scored United's only goal, Inter Milan made the then-astronomical offer of £65,000 for him, an offer Busby didn't even give serious consideration.

He liked his beer, but there was no more dedicated trainer and his genetic gifts allowed him to recover from having both cartilages out of each knee in an era when such an operation amounted to butchery.

Built like an Adonis, team-mates would recall the Yorkshireman polishing off a dozen bottles of lager, and then running at three-quarter pace in training next day, the sweat pouring off him until you could fill a bucket full of it. With curly black hair, winning smile and a jaunty self-belief, he had his share of female fans, one being David Pegg's sister, Irene.

'They all, David, Bob [Charlton] and Tommy, went to the dance halls together,' she said. 'I was very keen on Tommy until I realised he was a gobby bugger.'

He is buried at Monk Bretton cemetery in Barnsley. In July 2011 a blue plaque was unveiled (by Barnsley's own Dickie Bird) outside the Stretford lodging house where Taylor, Pegg and, before he married, Mark Jones lived. This was a heart-warming project by pupils at Stretford High School who produced a similar plaque to Duncan Edwards at his former lodgings in Gorse Avenue.

AT OLD TRAFFORD they called **MARK JONES** Dan Archer for his rural habits: shooting, country walks, his black Labrador Ric and his 55 budgies. He owned a shotgun to help keep the pigeon population under control at the ground and was one of the few Busby Babes to own a car, a Morris 1000 in which he ferried his wife June, pregnant with daughter Lynn at the time of Munich, and two-year-old Gary.

Jones, was only 24 at the time of Munich but seen as the elder statesman. He wore a trilby, smoked a pipe and the scar tissue and taut skin around his eyebrows made him look like a rather unsuccessful boxer who had just spent five rounds with Mohammed Ali. He lived on King's Road with his wife June, a Barnsley girl he had met when he was 16 and had trained as a bricklayer before becoming a professional footballer.

He left Wombwell, Barnsley, in 1948 to cross the Pennines and was already a captain of England Boys when he arrived. He signed professional forms in 1950 and was the archetypal stopper. As with Bill Foulkes after him, Murphy had hammered home the principles of centre-

> **Team-mates would recall the Yorkshireman polishing off a dozen bottles of lager, and then running at three-quarter pace in training next day, the sweat pouring off him**

half play early on to Mark: 'Nothing fancy, just boot the bloody ball over the stand.'

He was to win two championship medals with United, and relished the physical challenge from centre-forwards built on similar lines: Nat Lofthouse of Bolton and Sunderland's Trevor Ford; these were games within a game. He had stern competition at Old Trafford, a continual battle for the centre-half spot with Jackie Blanchflower, who had been best man at his wedding. The Ulsterman edged selection for the 1957 FA Cup Final, but by the time of Munich, Jones had his place back and was playing the best football of his career.

He was a man, seemingly, loved by all.

I had met John Docherty in 2004, three years before he died in 2007, in his regular place, a large hotel cum restaurant in south Manchester. It was a popular hangout for people with United connections (two days later Matt Busby's son, Sandy, chose to meet me in the same hotel . . . and at the same table). Doherty, an original Busby Babe whose own playing career was finished by a knee injury at the age of 23 was one of three members of the Munich testimonial committee of 1998 (the others being PFA head-honcho Gordon Taylor and United European Cup winner David Sadler).

Doherty, a cigar smoker of passion, was on first-name terms with most of the hotel staff and good company. But, like many Mancunians, he could be impulsive and alarmingly candid at times (a day after the interview he phoned me at home to ask to delete some of the tape, which I did). He liked to see himself as a hard-bitten old trooper – 'I don't get sentimental because I am an old man now' – but finished the interview thus: 'My eldest lad is called Mark after Mark Jones. He was a big, lovely fellow and every time I close my eyes I can always see Mark Jones's face. He was not a mate of mine, I was closer to the others, but he epitomised everything that was nice, everything that was good. He was a giant of a man and a giant of a human being. I loved him to bits.'

> **" I was closer to the others, but he epitomised everything that was nice, everything that was good. He was a giant of a man and a giant of a human being. I loved him to bits**

Večera u restoranu hotela "Majestic"
Dinner at hotel "Majestic" restaurant

The last word should go to June, who re-married, and wrote this to me in 2003: 'Mark was a lovely man, kind, honest and a great husband and dad. We were only together four and a half years. He went to Manchester United when he was about 16, but I didn't take much notice at the time because it was the man I was interested in not the football. Sometimes I wish he had never played and maybe he would still be with me and the family, the son he knew for two and a half years and the daughter he never knew and his four grandchildren

This extraordinary photograph still adorns a wall in the lobby of the Majestic Hotel in Belgrade. It was taken on the night of February 5, 1958. Busby and his players had just finished dinner not long after after the 3-3 draw with Red Star that had secured them a European Cup semi-final with AC Milan. Busby is offering some dos and donts and the local etiquette before his boys are let loose on the town. The un-named man on Busby's left is his third-in-command Bill Whalley, who was also to die at Munich next day. There's not a lot else to say, is there?

who he would have loved. He only wanted a family and of course to play football but what did football get him? Killed at 24. He had all his life in front of him and never got to live it. He has two grandsons, Mark who is called after him and Wayne and two granddaughters, Lisa and Laura, I know he would have been so proud of and he has never had the joy of seeing them grow up. Lyn never knew him and Gary was only two and a half so he doesn't remember him. Mark is buried just down the road from where we live and I can visit him when I want, which is two or three times a week. We didn't want the life these footballers have today, we would have been happy in our semi in Manchester. I've never been to a football match since; I can't and won't go because it would be Mark and all the ones he played with I would see, not the players of today. I have a sad day every 6 February and I'm not fit to talk to on that day so I just go to the grave with some flowers and sit there awhile. It has been 44 years but I am not going to forget him.'

> **Edwards warned Jackie Milburn: 'I don't care about reputations, they mean nothing to me. Any bother from you and I'll boot you over the stand.'**

HE BLUSHED WHEN his team-mates pulled his leg – usually about his Midlands accent and his birthplace of 'Dood-lie' – and as a boy kept pigeons and rabbits and liked fishing and hop-picking. But on his first visit as an England international to Hampden Park in April 1956, **DUNCAN EDWARDS** kicked the native icon Bobby Johnstone up in the air in front of screaming Scots. He warned the legendary Newcastle and England centre-forward Jackie Milburn (cousin of Bobby Charlton's mum no less) before a First Division match: 'I don't care about reputations, they mean nothing to me. Any bother from you and I'll boot you over the stand.' Afterwards, he told the bemused Milburn: 'Thanks for the game, chief.' He called everyone chief.

He was born on 1 October 1936, at 23 Malvern Crescent in Dudley before his parents, Sarah and Gladstone,

Here's the new boy showing off his square knit tie: It's August 1952 and Duncan Edwards from Dudley had just signed for Manchester United. Many in Dudley assumed he would join Wolves, or even Aston Villa, but in the end none could match the Old Trafford talent-gathering machine. Late in 1948 Midlands scout Jack O'Brien had written to Busby: 'Have today seen a schoolboy who merits special watching.' Late on 1 June, Bert Whalley drove assistant manager Jimmy Murphy, who didn't drive, through the night, arriving at the Edwards' home in the early hours. The sleep-befuddled boy, still in his pyjamas, signed there and then.

moved to Priory Estate, parts of which now are still considered the roughest and most deprived in the Midlands.

Duncan was ten when a sister, christened Carol Anne, died from meningitis at the age of ten weeks; he was to grow up healthy and strong and with good genes possibly inherited from his mum who, when she died in 2003, was 93 years old. His father played football at amateur level and an uncle was on Bolton's books in the early 30s and also represented England.

'Duncan the athlete came out of his mum,' said Albert Scanlon who was very good on football history. 'There was one time when we were doing laps and there was a lad called Alan Rhodes there. He was a gymnast, and could do double somersaults. Course, Duncan has to have a go. He falls flat on his arse the first time; the second time he does it, no problem.'

As with so many of the Busby Babes he had kicked a ball about from an early age, usually around Netherton or Priory Park. He played for Priory Road junior school, bossing the other boys around and at the age of 11 a watching schoolteacher wrote to a friend that he had seen a schoolboy 'who would one day play for England'.

For Matt Busby (and almost everyone else who saw him play) Duncan was 'the player who had everything': so big, so strong, and so confident, so young. It was impossible to spot flaws.

His death impacted into many areas, and not just among fans. His former England team-mate, Jimmy Armfield (who named his eldest son Duncan), said: 'He was a one-off and he grew up very quickly, he was physically mature at 18. When he first appeared for Young England, the opposition didn't dare tackle him. They just backed off. He was a super bloke but he liked his own way and could be fiery. But there is no doubt in my mind that with Byrne, Edwards and Taylor in the team we would have won the World Cup in Sweden in 1958 and in South America four years later. England

The usual routine the day before a match at Old Trafford was the dreaded photo shoots with local snappers allowed into the ground. Three of the regular targets were Duncan, right, Roger Byrne and, naturally, the boss himself. Cameramen also liked images of Duncan leaping the picket fences behind him! This was taken on 1 November 1957 and a goal from Tommy Taylor gave United a 1–0 win against Burnley next day.

United goalkeeper Ray Wood could command an area as he demonstrates to Bill Foulkes, left, Duncan and, hovering in the background Real maestro Alfredo Di Stefano. It was the second leg of the European Cup semi-final at Old Trafford on 25 April 1957 and it finished 2–2 (Real 5–3 on aggregate). It was rumoured that Edwards had so impressed Di Stefano (not a man noted for praising anyone) that he told his president he should tempt Edwards to Madrid.

could have had a hat-trick of World Cup wins. Munich robbed us of three of the greatest players of any era, not just the Babes era.'

The former England manager Terry Venables had been standing in the old Clock End at Highbury with his father, Fred, when United bade their unforgettable farewell to England five days before Munich. Venables, who was 15 at the time, recalled: 'When I was growing up, there was no televised football to speak of, and if you wanted to see a particular player or team, it meant going to one of their matches. It was February 1958 and United had just caused a stir by beating Bolton 7–2, and everyone was talking about Duncan Edwards. So I persuaded my dad to come with me to Highbury to see United play Arsenal. It was a day I will never forget. I couldn't take my eyes off Duncan. There were nine goals in a fantastic

If Duncan looks a little miffed then no wonder: United had just lost 4–1 at home to Cardiff on 4 April 1953 and this on his debut! United's only reply was a Roger Byrne penalty four minutes from time.

match, but Duncan was all I really remember.'

Good as he was, Duncan's Old Trafford team-mates made sure he never got too big for his boots.

Albert Scanlon said: 'After training we used to play a practice game. Bill Inglis, who liked to sneak off somewhere quiet for a smoke, says to us: "Go out there and do some laps until I'm ready for you." So Duncan puts his top on, two towels round his neck, and sets off. We did a few laps and then went back to the game. That's when we realised they were one short, and of course it's Duncan. He's still out there running. When he finally appears after about 30 minutes Bill says: "Where the hell have you been?" and Duncan says: "No one told me to stop."'

'Duncan only wanted one thing and that was to play football,' said Harry Gregg. 'At the end of every training session he would argue that we hadn't done enough yet. He didn't want to go in.'

Despite his apparent lack of guile, Edwards was well aware of the commercial opportunities his name and talent afforded him; in so many ways he was far ahead of his time. He had endorsed Dextrosol glucose tablets acclaiming a 'natural source of energy you can rely on anytime and anywhere' – not that he ever appeared to need any extra help – and had already acquired sponsored transport, a Raleigh racing bike. He was paid £4 10s a week by the *Manchester Evening Chronicle* for a newspaper column in the *Saturday Pink* and by the age of 21 had written a best-selling instructional book entitled *Tackle Soccer This Way*. Wise and far-sighted beyond his years he told one journalist: 'You can't live for ever on cheers; it's what you have in the bank at the end of the day that counts. People forget very quickly and I don't want to become like some of the old-timers wearing tattered caps and cadging for tickets outside the grounds.'

As it happened, fate spared Edwards decrepitude

> **Duncan only wanted one thing and that was to play football. At the end of every training session he would argue that we hadn't done enough yet**

and poverty, but also ensured that people would never forget. His stature since his death has grown rather than diminished.

On the day of his funeral 50,000 people lined the streets of the town and solemn, uniformed policemen saluted as the cortege drove slowly past.

His mother Annie kept three framed photographs on the living room wall: Duncan in his army uniform, one with his girlfriend Molly Leach, a Manchester girl he met on one of his afternoon trips to Ringway airport and one of him in the Manchester United jersey, the one in which he made his senior debut. She is buried in the churchyard alongside Gladstone, her daughter Carol and Duncan.

The town of Dudley has always ensured its favourite son will never be forgotten. There's a visitor trail to show various landmarks: a blue plaque in Priory Park, two stained-glass windows in St Francis Church (where Matt Busby took part in the dedication on 27 August 1961), his grave in Dudley Cemetery, a statue in the town centre, a Duncan Edwards Games Area, again in Priory Park, a Duncan Edwards Close and a Duncan Edwards Way.

THE CULLING

FIELDS

Busby says farewell – and thank you – to Professor Georg Maurer, chief physical at Rechts der Isar hospital in Munich. Busby had made a remarkable recovery and was discharged nine weeks after the accident.

It never seemed right to see Albert Scanlon in a Newcastle jersey. The Tyneside management obviously felt the same way for Scanlon was soon on the sporting spiral downwards: Lincoln, Mansfield and, finally, non-league Belper Town.

eeting Albert Scanlon for the first time was like a chapter from a Le Carré novel. To contact him I have to call a friend between 10 and 11am and then ring the same number again the following day when the meeting would be set up. By all accounts one of his daughters had put a block on his telephone.

He had suggested Pendleton Church on Broad Street as a rendezvous, though his home in Salford was less than a mile away and it would have been easier to get there.

'Typical Albert that,' said Harry Gregg when I recounted the story to him later. In the end I found him waiting, muffled by cap and coat, in the overgrown graveyard. He didn't look round as I approached.

'Cuppa tea?' he said, finally.

The council house smelled of damp and cigarette smoke and I had to put 50p in the electricity meter. There was no refrigerator. None of this bothered Albert in the slightest. He did have a new, wide-screen television, though, bought with part of his payment from the Munich testimonial fund. Some of the other proceeds (£300 in all) went to the Omagh bomb appeal and the family of the Coventry City steward crushed by a coach, both events taking place in 1998.

'Albert has always been a giver, never a taker,' said Gregg.

Scanlon lived alone, although he had a partner, two former wives and seven children. One was a policeman in Liverpool and 'there's another daughter in Los Angeles or somewhere'.

He was born in the Manchester suburb of Hulme in November 1935 in a house with two bedrooms, close by the old gasworks. The accommodation was shared by 15 others, including the four brothers and seven sisters of his father. Hulme, once known as Little Ireland, in the 30s and 40s had changed little from Victorian days when it was considered one of the worst slums in Europe. An upbringing in a place like that tends to make you streetwise but, in Albert Scanlon's case at least, open and magnanimous.

Gregg and several others I spoke to thought the world of him. 'When I had the hotel in Portstewart he would come across and everyone loved him,' said Gregg. 'Once when he was over he fancied a night out on his own so I left him in Coleraine, which is a very big town, and he found his way back home to Portstewart. Yes, Albert was always around . . . and so laid back he would fall over.'

He was an original Busby Babe but not a Busby type at all and Gregg gave one clue as to why Scanlon (and others) didn't survive an Old Trafford career very long after Munich.

'A year after the crash we flew to Rotterdam to play Feyenoord about the time Scanny had been picked for England B. It was the first flight after Munich for a lot of them. Ian Greaves cried off and (Bill) Foulkes was in a bad way going over. We landed in Rotterdam and I was rooming with Scanny. Tricky (Dennis) Viollet, of course, had imported his own bird from England.

'I never drank, but we were in a night club in Rotterdam and the thing with Matt Busby was that if the lads were in a club and he was there they would buy him a drink and then get the hell out of there, and vice versa. So that's what we did. But I remember outside this night club holding Scanny upright and the boss came out and said to me: "Goodnight Big Fella." Albert was spewing up. He is getting up at 7am that morning to go and play for England and the last I saw of him he was laying stretched out on his bed, like a corpse, and with a bunch of lilies in his hand. Next morning when I got up he was gone, back to England. He was man of the match at Highbury.'

'I get by these days,' he told me without a hint of

Matt and wife Jean arrive home at Kings Road, Chorlton-cum-Hardy, on 18 April 1958, to be met by daughter Sheena. By the end of the year Busby was ready to take the helm again. His injuries were to limit him to the manager's office for much of the week but that at least gave him the chance to build a squad capable of challenging for honours again. For various reasons many of the Munich survivors wouldn't be involved in the manager's new United.

● The *Mirror* photographer had been on a mission to catch the Manchester United WAGS on their way to Moscow for the Champions League Final against Chelsea in May 2008.

He also got Albert Scanlon, one of the great nomads of British football, who had been invited on to the same private jet to Russia, along with fellow Munich survivors Charlton, Gregg and Foulkes.

At Old Trafford his nickname was Joe Friday, as in the police lieutenant from *Dragnet*, the American TV series who always favoured a white raincoat.

Scanlon also liked to dress in white, though he disputed the source of his nickname: 'It was because I was always around whenever something was going off.' Scanlon died of kidney problems (he had suffered kidney damage in the air crash) and pneumonia in December 2009.

remorse. 'But people do tend to think that if you have won a championship or the cup that's enough. At least I've got my memories.'

He had indeed. He had a gift for almost total recall and a habit (something I always thought unique to Mancunians) of deliberately side-tracking a main story with extended detail before heading back to the original. Thus, on his early days at United, circa 1952, was fairly typical: 'The lads spent seven days a week training and the first time I saw tracksuits Bert Whalley had a purple one on and Jimmy Murphy a green one on. Some days, when the first team was away, we would just sit in the stand. They had just put the new stand up and there was just a shed at the Warwick Road end. The main stand, there were two fellows painting it. Jim and Barney painted everything that didn't move at Old Trafford, just the two of them. They'd paint you if you stood still long enough. Their gaffer was named George and he was from Wythenshawe. Once I came out to see a ball sitting on the pitch. Then

this fellah who looked familiar came out and he spent half an hour hitting the ball, taking corners, hitting penalties at both ends of the pitch. He had a black-and-white top on, and I found out later it was because he wasn't supposed to be there. At the end he picked the ball up, marched to the centre circle, looked round and then booted this ball way up into the sky, turned round, trapped it with his arse and then marched off like a sergeant major out of the ground. Then he got in his car and drove off.

'I said to Bill Inglis: "Who was that?"

'And Bill says: "Charlie Mitten."'

SCANLON'S PLAYING apprenticeship had mirrored that of virtually every other working-class youngster growing up in the 40s and 50s. On one 'field' he played on in Hulme at one end there was a bombed fire station, at the other a bombed swimming baths.

Hulme was City territory and there they used to

Long before the days of instant replay some canny work by a *Mirror* snapper and caption writer on 11 February 1950, as Manchester United and Portsmouth battle out a 3–3 draw in an FA Cup match at Old Trafford. Stan Pearson heads United's second off a corner by Charlie Mitten. Local lad Mitten was a member of Busby's first great side after the war and later, famously, a defector to a team in Colombia where, by all accounts, he made a small fortune. If Albert did have any idols in his early days at Old Trafford, Mitten was certainly one of them.

Charlie takes on Manchester City's most famous German, Bert Trautmann, in a First Division match at Maine Road in December 1949. United won 2–1 in the end.

'laugh at United'. He said: 'I can recall their first trophy win after the war. They beat Accrington Stanley 4–1 in the Lancashire Cup and there was Johnny Carey stood on the steps at Maine Road with this little trophy and no one was really bothered 'cos it was United. But I was. Johnny Carey had come to our school once and he went through the usual routine of asking us all what we wanted to do when we grew up. I piped up: "I want to play for United," and they all laughed, Carey included. But I did in the end. Within a few years I was laying out Carey's kit in the first-team dressing room.'

One afternoon, towards the end of another boys' game at the end of 1950, Scanlon noticed 'another fellah sat in

an overcoat watching us. At the end he said: "I've come to ask you a question: Would you like to sign for Manchester United? I am going to tell you the same as we tell everyone else. We think we can make a footballer out of you, but we are not going to promise anything. What do you say, here and now?" I said "Yes". It was Jimmy Murphy and so I was one of the first Busby Babes . . . and one of the lucky ones as it turned out.'

Many of the survivors were bitter, though Scanlon remained pragmatic and more mindful of others to the end.

'Jackie Blanchflower and Johnny Berry found life very hard after Munich and I was very disappointed with

All had been forgiven when Charlie Mitten arrived back in Britain after his sojourn in Colombia and though United were never going to invite him back, Newcastle United did, appointing him manager in 1958. Charlie was in his 40s when this was taken in 1960 but the Toon manager looks fit and still able to teach his dogs new tricks!

United,' he said. 'At least I played 40 games for them after the crash. I played half the next season, we got knocked out of the cup by Norwich and Matt told me he was putting Bobby Charlton in for the next friendly against City which United won 3–1. Matt basically cut us off and I thought he was getting rid of what was left from Munich. Tricky (Dennis) Viollet did a great job for the club, but Matt eventually sold him to Stoke City and he never got a benefit.

'To my mind, Munich killed not only a lot of the players who were on that flight, but some of the survivors, too, and all the young players who had to come in a year or two too early. They were never the same. Things changed for all time at Munich and United didn't come up to par. The two men I blame for it are dead now and that's Busby and Louis Edwards, who was made chairman just after the crash. They make a show of '58 when it suits them.

'When I went to Newcastle Matt made a promise and never kept it. He told me that financially I would be all right (according to Gregg, Busby had made a similar promise to Kenny Morgans when the winger was sold on to his hometown club Swansea). Matt met me at the Midland Hotel at 11 o'clock at night, and drove me to the Queens. He told me it was best I had a break and left Manchester. "Don't worry, I'll fix all the financial things for you." Five years later I saw him outside the ground and he didn't want to know me.'

MUNICH HAD left Dennis Viollet seemingly unscathed, although many were to remark that his personality changed drastically. 'I think he realised that life was worth more than football,' said John Doherty. 'He got in with a different crowd after Munich and it came down to a simple thing with Dennis: either he was boss or Matt [Busby] was boss. In the end there was only going to be one winner. Matt got rid of him because he thought him a bad example to kids. I think after the experience of Munich Dennis was

Dennis at his best, leaping to score the third goal (and his hat-trick) in Manchester United's 3–2 defeat of Preston in August 1956. The Old Trafford smog was something you soon got used to!

Under the circumstances Manchester United had done remarkably well to reach the final of the FA Cup at Wembley in May 1958. Busby arrived on crutches, Charlton sat in the stand, but United were no match for Bolton and their superstar Nat Lofthouse (who performed a replay and of the '57 final and bundled Harry Gregg over the line for a winner). It was also remarkable to find Dennis Viollet back in action, 86 days after a crash that left him with a bang on his head and facial injuries. Here he is beaten to a cross by the diminutive Bolton goalkeeper Eddie Hopkinson, a '5ft 8in colossus' as one Bolton supporter described him to me once.

There was something symbolic and (for me at least) deeply sad about this image of new King of Old Trafford Denis Law giving a former United hero and striking buccaneer Dennis Viollet a consolatory pat on the head after Law's four goals helped United to a 5–2 win over Stoke City on 7 December 1963. Old maestro Stan Matthews, left, is obviously in a hurry.

determined to lead life to the full and that was a life that didn't necessarily square up with being a top-class athlete. He was moved on before he was finished as a footballer.'

Eventually, in the summer of 1961, Busby sold him to Stoke where he enjoyed a glorious Indian summer to his career before an even more remarkable spell in the United States. His marriage to Barbara had failed to stand the test of time. They had married when Dennis was 17 and Barbara pregnant with their first son, Roger (yet another boy named after Roger Byrne).

Helen Greeph, his second wife, always reminded me of one of those many spectacularly beautiful Jewish girls I would see in Heaton Park most weekends: dark looks, talkative and with unabashed candour. Helen tended to make an impression, too: 'It was a year after the crash and a Jewish Association do at Sale Locarno,' recalled Albert Scanlon. 'There was this girl in charge of the tombola and I remember her swaying through the crowd in an emerald green dress and with no shoes on.'

● Some words of advice from Waddington for Viollet and the famed hard man Maurice Setters in January 1967. This was the day before Stoke's 0–2 FA Cup third round defeat by Manchester United at Old Trafford, both Viollet and Setters being ex-United players by then.

Waddington, affable and articulate, was one of the great characters of the game and a match at the Victoria Ground, drinks with Waddington (and a visit to the nearby nightclub) was very popular (and far more entertaining than games at Old Trafford) with football reporters in the 60s.

Waddington, a great wheeler-dealer, was noted for his signings of the cast-offs and veterans considered being past their prime, among them the galloping grandad Stanley Matthews, George Eastham OBE, Peter Dobie and, of course, Busby rejects Viollet and Setters. Unlike United, Stoke granted Viollet a testimonial when he left in May 1967.

Stoke City manager Tony Waddington (left) with new signing Dennis Viollet in January 1962.

'I met Dennis when I was 16 and I used to see him around town after that,' Helen said during a lengthy call to her home in the United States. 'Once, in the New Theatre Bar, I was chatting with Dennis and Marlene Shapiro, Bobby Charlton's ex-girlfriend. Marlene was madly in love with Dennis, who carried on just like a single fellow. But I was determined not to be charmed by him. I had a boyfriend at the time and he wouldn't let me meet him. He kept me in the car because he said I would fall for him as all the women did. And it's true, men and women were so attracted to him. He was also determined to enjoy every minute of the life that was left to him.'

It was a difficult situation for both. She was involved with a married man and still living at home. She got a job in Blackpool demonstrating in a department store and Viollet would drive over two or three times a week.

'My dad was a really rigid disciplinarian and eventually I left home and got a job as one of the Living Fire Girls.'

They were married in September 1969 and bought a property on Cherry Tree Road, Wythenshawe, but life after playing proved difficult. He got a job with Preston coaching, played a season for Linfield then had a disastrous spell with Crewe Athletic.

'We really struggled then,' said Helen. 'He had to sign on the dole and there seemed to be nothing on the horizon. But then someone phoned and asked if we would go to America. We came back here in March 1973 and were at Baltimore, Columbia, Maryland and Washington Diplomats. At Boston, Noel Cantwell was in charge and then the franchise was moved to Jacksonville, where Gerry Daly, Peter Simpson and Keith Weller also played. We had wonderful times, had a lot of fun, and then bought a house in Foxborough. This is where he built his wonderful reputation, the community thought the world of him. Dennis always had a great feeling for Jewish people. There was no religion in our life, but if anyone said anything anti-Semitic he would just blow up. He had been to Auschwitz and Belsen. He stayed pally with all the boys. Greggy he was very fond of but was always saying: "He's mad, he's wild."'

It was actually Gregg who first spotted the decline in Viollet's health and his ultimate brain tumour. In 1997 the '58 survivors had been invited to Munich for the European Cup Final between Juventus and Borussia Dortmund (this at the invitation of UEFA).

Gregg recalled: 'They booked me into Manchester airport before the flight out next day and that night the hotel room phone rang: "Greggy, it's me Tricky." He came up to my room and there he was. Now Dennis was a man who was immaculate on the field and off it, but he was a mess in an old American-style pullover. He stood there and he said: "You are looking well," and I said: "So are you" and I thought: who's the biggest liar? The way he talked was all funny and he wanted to buy everyone drinks, with American money.'

The following day the party flew to Frankfurt and half an hour after they had arrived Viollet had vanished.

Gregg added: 'When I caught up with the rest of the lads at Bayern's old ground I said to them: "There is something desperately wrong with Tricky." Then he got lost at the game and got the wrong flight home to America, by all accounts. When Helen rang up and told us the worst I mentioned the knock he got on his head at Munich and she was screaming: "That's where the tumour was."'

Like many survivors of that Munich flight (and many of their family members, too) Viollet had dreaded 6

> **Men and women were so attracted to him. He was also determined to enjoy every minute of the life that was left to him**

February, every year. Helen recalled: 'He would say: "Is it 6 February today?" He always got a funny feeling on 6 February. He was a very private person but he did open up after a drink and probably if I'm honest I would admit he did drink a little bit too much. Once he started he would consume a fair amount. One particular night he started talking about it. When he became ill, the February after that was the 40th anniversary and Dennis started to cry: "I'll never see them again, Duncan and Eddie and Roger." What happens with a brain tumour is that your long-term memory becomes very sharp. He never used to cry but he became very emotional when he was ill.

'I don't know what I would have done without that money from the Munich testimonial because he had no insurance – the renewal date was just after he fell ill – and we had used up all our savings on his treatment. You can't go through life feeling bitter about it. The club helped. When he was sick I wrote to them and they sent $10,000, twice. Martin Edwards came to Dennis's memorial service at Old Trafford and was charming. Ken Merritt, the secretary, had always been very helpful. But it was all I had to live on for the rest of my life. Dennis adored America, we laughed all the time, and it was a really fun marriage. I have been very lucky, and I don't think I would have got married if I hadn't met Dennis. I was bowled over by him; luckily it seemed to go the other way, too.

'What he did for the kids in this area. There was one boy called Dylan who had only one arm and Dennis adored him and vice versa. We sold all his medals and memorabilia and raised about $10,000 for it. At the end of January, I thought he had Alzheimer's. He started to forget things and he was not like that, he was always very neat and tidy but that went by the board. Once he went to the loo in a local restaurant and couldn't remember his way back to the table. He started feeling dizzy and then saying he could smell a sweet smell. He went away with

Dennis in celebratory mood with his Stoke team-mates Don Ratcliffe and Eric Skeels after the 2–0 win over Luton Town on 18 May 1963. His 23 goals that season (including four against Charlton) helped Stoke win promotion to the First Division after a ten-year absence.

the team, Team Cyclone, in 1997 and I got a phone call in the middle of the night: "Coach is not well, Mrs Viollet. He thinks he is back in Jacksonville and he kept turning and walking away during our game."'

He had a brain scan and it was discovered there were lesions on his brain. Then a biopsy found the tumour.

'They got most of the tumour, but we knew it was terminal. He had a bleed to his brain, more surgery to remove clots, which lasted 24 hours, but he never walked again. There was chemotherapy and radiation and in January and February of 1998 he started to improve and began to walk a bit with help. He got presented with the key to the city of Jacksonville, which was very touching, but then he started to deteriorate and they told me it had spread. Then came the last birthday, in September, the last Thanksgiving, the last Christmas, the last day in St Augustine, and the last three weeks of life. Dennis died, listening to Mozart and with Rachel and myself holding his hand. Not a bad way to leave this world when you think about it.'

Viollet's qualities were inherited by his youngest daughter Rachel, whose abilities on a tennis court made her British No.1 (and an appearance at Wimbledon) in 1996.

KENNY MORGANS made a full recovery from his Munich injuries and was playing again before the end of 1958. But his ability to take on defenders and dominate his wing seemed to have gone. According to Albert Scanlon Busby had promised the Welshman he 'would be all right financially' (the same pledge he had made to Scanlon) but he was sold to his hometown club, Swansea City, in 1961. It left him, along with most of the other Munich survivors and families, deeply embittered by the club's indifference to their fates. 'Young Kenny' as Harry Gregg always insisted on calling him, was 73 when he died in 2012.

Happier times for Ray Wood and his wife Elizabeth as they relax in the team hotel a day before the Wembley Cup final against Aston Villa.

Jackie Blanchflower and Ray Wood kill time on the flight to Spain and the European Cup semi-final against Real Madrid on 11 April 1957. Cheeky chappie Eddie Colman looks on.

RAY WOOD, Gregg's predecessor in the United goal, was noted for his bravery and agility but is still probably better known as the victim of the assault by Aston Villa forward Peter McParland, six minutes into the FA Cup Final at Wembley in 1957. The tackle – deemed a fair challenge by BBC commentator Kenneth Wolstenholme – left Wood unconscious and with a broken cheekbone, all far worse than the damage he suffered at Munich. McParland, who was to win 34 caps with Northern Ireland, wisely stayed on the ground until it was obvious the referee wasn't going to take any action.

With no substitutes allowed in those days Jackie Blanchflower took over in goal. McParland scored both Villa goals in the 2–1 victory while Wood, with astonishing bravery, returned to the pitch . . . on the wing. He used to tell an amusing story about how, having regained consciousness, he was told to warm up in a Wembley car park where a young boy with a football had asked if he 'fancied a kickabout'.

As for the villain of the piece, he was soon forgiven, according to Joy Byrne. She was on honeymoon with Roger in Jersey a month after the final – and at the same time as Jackie and Jean Blanchflower – when they came

upon Peter McParland on the island. 'They all got on like a house on fire,' said Joy.

After the disastrous cup final and Munich eight months later he never managed to oust Gregg and Busby soon moved him on to Huddersfield and from there he joined Bradford and Barnsley before qualifying as an FA coach. Later he enjoyed an amazing nomadic career which took in coaching in America, Cyprus, Greece, Canada, Kuwait, Kenya, the UAR and Zambia. He returned to Britain in 1982 to settle in Bexhill-on-Sea in Sussex and, like former Old Trafford team-mate Bill Foulkes, took up golf with a vengeance. He ran a sportswear business in Bexhill, then took charge of a suit department for a store in Hastings before retirement in the mid-1990s. Wood, a regular smoker, had already survived one heart attack before his death in the summer of 2002.

His first marriage to Elizabeth had ended in divorce. His name, as the names of Munich survivors often do, surfaced in the newspapers again shortly before he died when he fell out with his local golf club over their insistence that club officials should wear a gold-and-navy-striped blazer. Wood, the club captain, refused because 'it makes me look like a cross between a deckchair attendant and an overgrown wasp. It also makes the club a laughing stock.'

At his funeral in East Sussex, in the summer of 2002, they played the Morecambe and Wise theme song 'Bring Me Sunshine' and a week later Debbie, one of his two daughters, sent Albert Scanlon a card which concluded with the words: 'Thanks for all the good times you had with dad.'

▲ The tackle by Peter McParland (above left) in the FA Cup Final at Wembley in 1957 – deemed a fair challenge by BBC commentator Kenneth Wolstenholme – left Wood unconscious and with a broken cheekbone.

◀ Stand-in goalkeeper Jackie Blanchflower holds off Aston Villa's Johnny Dixon during the infamous FA Cup Final against Aston Villa in May 1957. Bill Foulkes rides shotgun on the right with Duncan Edwards just out of sight behind Jackie.

Goalscorer Johnny Berry, Duncan Edwards and Matt Busby celebrate the 2–0 FA Cup semi-final win over Birmingham at Hillsborough in March 1957.

THERE WAS A FAMOUS story Harry Gregg told about the Manchester United assistant manager Jimmy Murphy escorting him and Bill Foulkes from Manchester to Rechts Isar Hospital in Munich to meet the chief surgeon, Dr Georg Maurer. Maurer, soon to be idolised by every Manchester United supporter, took the three on a tour of the wards containing their stricken team-mates. The surgeon went to each bed and gave his verdict: Busby and Edwards, 50-50, Jackie Blanchflower and Scanny, a thumbs up, Dennis Viollet, OK. When he got to Johnny Berry he sighed and said: "I am not God."

In the end there must have been a god somewhere for Berry, outwardly the smallest and frailest of the players, overcame the most fearful odds to survive. Like Blanchflower and some of the other survivors he paid a fearful price for his 'luck'.

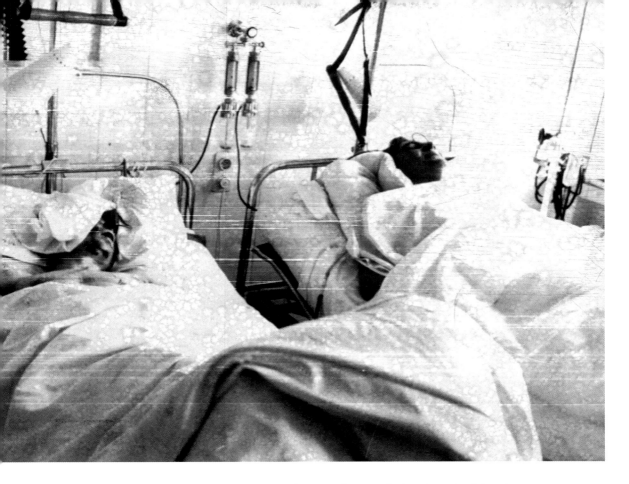

One year later all three were lying close to death in a Munich hospital bed. Both of the players were conscious but heavily sedated. Against all odds the smallest and frailest, Johnny Berry, survived; Duncan Edwards, the colossus, did not. Busby was in an oxygen tent and had been given the last rites. This was the 50s and apparently it was quite acceptable for images of the seriously ill (terminally ill in the case of Edwards) to appear in print.

Born in Aldershot on 1 June 1926, the winger had been rejected by his hometown team as 'too small to make a footballer', and when he left school it was to become a trainee cinema projectionist. But he went on to make 276 appearances for Birmingham City, his only other senior club, between 1951 and 1958. Like many of his team-mates, Berry played for the British Army team during the Second World War and his talents as a winger – pace, a shrewd football brain and the ability to get to the byline and deliver damaging crosses, caught the eye of Fred Harris, the Birmingham captain, who was in the same Army side in India.

> **Berry turned out to be one of their most successful buys ever, collecting three championship medals, four England caps and a cup final runners-up medal**

It was these talents, plus some memorable performances against his side in the First Division, that persuaded Busby, looking for a replacement for the ageing Jimmy Delaney, to splash out £27,000 to take him to Old Trafford in 1951. Berry, like Byrne, thus bridged the gap between the title-winning side of 1952 and the Babes of 1956.

Berry turned out to be one of their most successful buys ever, collecting three championship medals, four England caps and a cup final runners-up medal in 1957. His worth to the side is best summed-up by John Doherty: 'Someone like Beckham couldn't hold a candle to Johnny Berry. Beckham bends the ball and I say two things: a) I bet £100 he can't kick it straight because the ball is too light, and b) I'll give him an old-fashioned case ball and see how many times he scores with it. The ball swerves, he doesn't make it swerve. I look at Beckham and he can't go past anyone. I have never seen him beat anyone, he doesn't have the pace to do it; Giggs has all the pace in the world and his final ball is outrageous.

'Beckham is supposed to be the best crosser of the ball, and he's OK when he's got the time and space. But could he do it with the full-back tackling him? Johnny Berry could. Johnny could get to the byline and bend his toe round the ball. And he scored goals [45 in 276 appearances for United, including the winner in the quarter-final of the European Cup in 1957 against Athletic Bilbao]. When he was at Birmingham he used to make United's life a misery.'

Berry's injuries at Munich included a fractured skull, a broken jaw, injuries leading to the removal of all his teeth, a shattered elbow joint and a broken pelvis. Like Blanchflower and Busby, he was given the last rites by a German priest. He was in a coma for two months and when he did return to Manchester three months after the crash he knew nothing of it, or of the death of his team-mates. The Berry family's agonies, however, were just beginning. It was plain he would never play again, but a light had also gone out elsewhere.

Scanlon recalled a former players' dinner where 'Johnny was spilling his soup all down his chin' and Gregg said of the tiny winger's – he stood only 5ft 5ins and weighed under 10 stones – forlorn attempt to reintegrate himself at Old Trafford: 'His foot-eye co-ordination had gone, but still Johnny came down to Old Trafford, the little sick man, like a wee cock sparrow, to try and train with Jackie. It was pitiful. Johnny was so small and they couldn't tell him, or wouldn't tell him, that he had damaged this thing to his brain when he got the knock on his head.'

There was little in the way of compassion from Berry's employers. Within 12 months the Berry family, Johnny and Hilda along with their eight-year-old son Neil, had been ordered to leave their club house just off Davyhulme Road (to make way for Shay Brennan) and his employment cards arrived in a brown envelope through the post. He worked for a time as a labourer at Massey Harris in Trafford Park before returning to his home town of Aldershot, where he went into business with his younger brother Peter, another former professional footballer, selling sports clothing.

Neil, his son, who went on to a successful career as a head teacher in Buckinghamshire and later central London, was to give a hint of the family's sufferings when he said: 'My father went away to play football as one man and returned as a completely different person. He was never able to drive or concentrate for any length of time, and though as he grew older his injuries caused him increasing pain, he seldom complained. The Munich air crash changed the life of my family forever. We were all personally traumatised by it and suffered indescribable private grief.'

Given the reality of United's inability, or unwillingness, to help it was inevitable that Hilda Berry became extremely embittered.

She never forgot or forgave the club and the strength of her feelings is best illustrated by the fact that when her husband died in 1994, Harry Gregg had to telephone her and ask if it would be all right for the old players' association to send a bouquet of carnations – red and white carnations – to the funeral.

IN THE EARLY 90s Jackie Blanchflower had begun to write his life story. He managed only two or three chapters but his son, Andrew, still has the full, unfinished manuscript along with some tapes with random thoughts. The book was to open with Jackie lying in the snow at Munich airfield pinned to his seat by the body of his captain, Roger Byrne. Jackie wrote that while waiting for rescue he watched the second hand of Roger's wristwatch ticking away, the machinery still alive though its owner wasn't. Some would call that melodrama, the sort a writer would use to turn pages but Munich was but a part of one man's tragedy and one that still moves, and angers, me today.

As Laurie, one of his two daughters wondered a few years after her father's death in 1998: 'Were the ones that died the ones that got away with it?'

It was his Northern Ireland team-mate and friend Harry Gregg who found Blanchflower in the wreckage, his right arm badly broken and almost severed and his pelvis smashed. He suffered grievous renal damage, a factor that would shorten his life.

His son Andrew insisted: 'The papers said it was cancer, but it was acute liver failure in the end. I never saw him drink excessively, but he damaged a big part of it at Munich, and he only had one kidney. The legacy of Munich got them all in the end.'

Jackie had spent most of his life fighting long odds. Much of his career was spent in the shadow of his brother Danny and at Old Trafford he found himself in competition with Mark Jones at centre-half. But he had modified himself to cover many positions, most famously in the 1957 FA Cup Final when he had to take over in goal after Aston Villa's Peter McParland

Jackie Blanchflower cuts the cake on his wedding day with Jean on 7 July 1956.

Jackie Blanchflower preferred crossword puzzles to snooker – and always with the omnipresent boss, Matt Busby, close by.

had put Ray Wood out of the game. Such was Jackie's assuredness at Wembley he was selected as a goalkeeper on a club tour later; the ultimate utility player.

He was 15 when he arrived at Old Trafford from Northern Ireland, one of the first of the Babes, and by the time he was 22 he had won a league championship medal.

He wasn't totally devoted to football and, out of the eyes of manager Matt Busby, he took part in illegal boxing matches (with team-mate Tommy Taylor as his trainer and second). 'That was how he used to make extra money to send home to his mum in Northern Ireland,' said his son Andrew. 'Not that he ever made much because he never won. One day he had a bit of a shiner and he told Matt Busby he had walked into a door.'

As with so many others, Blanchflower's life was all about what might have been but for Munich. He would undoubtedly have fulfilled a lifetime's dream to have played for Northern Ireland in Sweden in the summer of 1958 alongside his brother Danny and Harry Gregg. And like many of the Munich survivors he was treated appallingly by Manchester United and, understandably, an affable man adored by all became quite bitter in the end. The club were clueless: it was decided that the families of players unlikely to have a future at Old Trafford were to vacate their club houses – with the exception of Joy Byrne, widow of the club captain.

True, Joy was soon to give birth to Roger Jnr at the time of Munich, but Jean Blanchflower was also pregnant, with her first daughter, Christa when ordered to find a new home . . . while Jackie went looking for a new job.

He bought a newspaper shop, worked for a bookmaker, moved into a pub, became a finance officer, all of them brought to an end by the run of bad luck that haunted him post-Munich. The feeling that the world had deserted him was only exacerbated by his former club.

'Jackie told me he never went back to Old Trafford because he was afraid of being turned away,' said Albert Scanlon. 'Once he went down, as we all have done, and tried to get a ticket and the kid in the ticket office, who was probably around 18 years old, didn't know him. Jackie had wanted two tickets for his doctor, but they turned him away. "That's why I never go back there," Jackie told me.'

Looking at the history of Old Trafford post-Munich, too, there's a recurring theme: female relatives of players involved in the crash despised Manchester United (some with a passion) but male counterparts adore the club (also with a passion).

● Jackie Blanchflower teaches his five-year-old son Andrew the tricks of the trade. Andrew, a Manchester United fan for life, was unaware of his father's place in the history of the club for a long time. It was only after Jackie took over the running of the Royal Oak at Millbrook, near Stalybridge, in 1968 – the year of the European Cup Final win – that customers began to remind him.

'To us he was just Dad,' said Andrew. 'He never came across as a celebrity and I don't think they were in those days. The celebrity he enjoyed was in the last ten years of his life and I think people made a fuss of him. People used to come into pub to see him.

'But "Jackie Blanchflower, Busby Babe" didn't mean anything to us. I remember going to the 20th centenary match in 1978 when I was about 15 and they were shouting his name, and he came on to the pitch and they were shouting "One Jackie Blanchflower" and I was so embarrassed. That's how I was with it. He stayed passionate about football, like anyone who has ever played. He would have played for nothing, which is what they did in them days. At work they would ask him: "Are you any relation to Danny?" and he would always say "no relation", and that was what Munich took away from him; the chance to be as big as his big brother. That team would have achieved it; he was part of something that was going to be really big. That was what he was bitter about. He never thought he got dealt a great hand. Munich was the start of a bad run for him. People used to say "you were lucky". Some luck.'

Matt Busby's modus operandi ahead of a big match on a Saturday was to take his squad to Davyhulme Park Golf Club for steaks all round and R&R: snooker, card games or just sitting around. The cast may have changed down the years, but Busby always kept to the same routine until the day he retired in 1969. This was taken in January 1955 and club golf pro Ken Geddes is demonstrating grips (with a snooker cue!) to Tommy Taylor, Don Gibson (soon to be sold to Sheffield Wednesday for £8k), Dennis Viollet, Jackie Blanchflower and Gunner Rowley (also close to the end of an illustrious playing career).

Andrew Blanchflower revealed in one moment that the club had demanded the return of his father's season ticket ('because he hardly uses it') and other slights 'which I would never tell you or anyone else about' and in the next admits: 'At the end of the day my dad played for the team I love and whether bad to him or not I still love them. I can't help that.'

His sister Laurie, like her mother before her, would argue that: 'Andrew was going to Old Trafford since he was four or five, but I don't like football at all. I don't understand it, and I don't want any connection with it. I have no time at all for Manchester United. The only thing I thank them for is that they wrote and said they would send a representative to my dad's funeral and I thought it would be the toilet cleaner, but it was Alex Ferguson. When I was a child because my name was Blanchflower people thought we were brought up with a silver spoon in our mouths. But Dad kept being made redundant. They would be cutting the water off and many times my mum's been hiding behind the settee from the bailiffs. I thought we were playing a game. Dad wasn't the luckiest. Mum used to say he used up all the family's luck surviving Munich.'

The Blanchflower children came to dread every 6 February. Laurie again: 'It was never a normal day and never a normal night and even the couple of days leading up to it were bad. Every time he shut his eyes he must have seen it. He wanted to be left alone with his memories, he wanted to be with the lads who died, he would rather have gone with them than never play again.'

'Every 6 February was a nightmare to us,' added Andrew. 'He used to say he wished he was dead with all his mates. It was a real bad time especially when we lived in the pub because he would have a drink and that worsens the problem. We used to keep away from him.'

When Jackie finally made it back to Old Trafford, this for the Munich memorial match (doubling as a crude 'farewell to Eric Cantona' celebration in August 1998) he

It was a case of making ends meet for Jackie and his family after Munich cut short his football career. He tried everything: a paper and sweet shop, a bookmaker and a pub landlord. He studied accountancy and became a popular after-dinner speaker.

had a month to live. Andrew said: 'At first I didn't want him to go [to the match] because we are making an exhibition of a dying man and that's not fair. But once we had got there it was all right.'

Laurie disagreed: 'The memorial turned into a pity thing and I don't think they did enough for them in the end. The club could have doubled it, no problems. They have ridden on that tragedy; it has made them what they are today.'

Jackie and Jean got their elusive break in the mid-80s. Jean had been quite well known as a singer on the club scene in the 50s and in an effort to keep the wolves from the door she returned to her old job, mainly in working mens' clubs. Jackie decided to go along with her to do the introductions, a decision that sparked a successful career as an after-dinner speaker.

'Mum said she couldn't get him off the stage in the end,' said Laurie. 'But he never really looked back, and he was a very funny man. He didn't do men only; he was very moralistic and shy. I never heard him say the f-word.'

Jackie died on 1 September 1998, but the family's run of ill fortune continued. Jean developed a circulatory problem and eventually both legs had to be amputated and, ultimately, a fatal heart attack. Laurie was convinced that 'when Dad went half my mum died, too. They were inseparable. I think she just gave up in the end. It was such a shame because things could have been so different. Dad was at that stage where he was turning into a really nice old man, really caring, making a fuss of the kids, his grandchildren. It robbed them of that. I think he liked being recognised, just going to the working men's club on Saturday. He had time for everybody. I never heard anyone say they didn't like my dad.

Another famous Blanchflower, the captain of the Spurs double side Danny, leads the way out of St Martin's in the Field church in Trafalgar Square after a memorial service for the Munich disaster victims.

'At least he did make it back for the 1998 testimonial and it was good for him to see his old team-mates. But it was also very sad because it was too late for him. If they had done something like that years before I'm not saying he wouldn't have died; I am just saying he would have had a better life. Families have had to suffer, too. We have had to suffer. United didn't do enough, but could you ever do enough for them? How do you put a price on something like that?'

Laurie christened her son Jack Blanchflower Barton: 'Someone thought we were sad. They thought it was because we supported United, but I thought it was one way of remembering Dad.'

DON'T CALL ME A HERO

When I met him in 2002 Gregg was living in a large, converted farmhouse on the Co. Antrim coast. There were horses in a field behind the main building and some land. He had just had two operations for removal of a bowel tumour and his runs along the local strand had slowed to walks. He had mistaken the day of the interview but allowed me in anyway. He was affable and talkative but unsmiling and with a definite feeling that this was not a man to argue with. Some said that after Munich he'd vowed never to be caught smiling in public in case a camera caught

Harry Gregg faces the Press four days after the Munich disaster.

Happy birthday for eight-year-old Linda from dad Harry, mum Carolyn and lots of friends in October, 1965.

Gregg with new bride Carolyn Maunders at St Mary's Parish Church, Rostherne, in July 1965, watched by bridesmaids Karen and Linda, his daughters. Gregg was still a Doncaster Rovers player when he married his first wife, Mavis Markham in 1957. Mavis died of cancer in 1961 as did 50-year-old Karen in 2009.

It was all fair in love and war back then when a centre-forward can simply charge a goalkeeper over the line and get away with it; as did Nat Lofthouse scoring his second against Harry Gregg at Wembley in 1958.

Nat Lofthouse, the Lion of Vienna, was the bane of United (and many other teams) in the 50s but particularly in the FA Cup Final in May 1958. Gregg lies stricken as Lofthouse opens the scoring in Bolton's 2–0 win. Stan Crowther, wearing a No.6 jersey, isn't much help either.

him and twisted the image in the way newspapers do. Bobby Charlton adopted a similar mourning appearance post-58, but there are still hundreds of images of a happy teenager enjoying life. It would be hard to find a smile from Harry Gregg anywhere and at any time.

'If Harry likes you you'll never know,' Albert Scanlon had warned me. 'But if he dislikes you'll soon find out.'

When we met, his autobiography, *Harry's Game*, had just been published, parts of it focusing on his allegations that some United players took bribes in the 1960s. He didn't name names, but a telephone rang constantly in another room throughout the four hours I spent with him. He ignored them.

His road to Old Trafford came via Coleraine, Linfield

Manchester City's Joe Hayes challenges Gregg at Maine Road on 19 September 1959. Bolton-born Hayes finished up with two goals (with a third from George Hannah). Gregg's opposite number was former Axis paratrooper Bert Trautmann, by then in his tenth season with City (with another five to go). Wilf McGuinness is the United player in the centre of the screen with the blond hair of Albert Quixall unmistakable to the left.

and Doncaster Rovers. A joiner by trade, he had signed for Doncaster to join his great countryman, and boyhood hero, Peter Doherty, who at the time was manager at Belle Vue. Doncaster were not the minnows of today – there were floodlights long before Manchester United – and he had made his first-team debut early in 1953 against Blackburn Rovers. At one stage he had charged out of goal to wipe out opposing centre-forward Tommy Briggs . . . and a Doncaster defender. All goalkeepers are crazy, as the old football adage goes. When he arrived in Manchester, in December 1957, thanks to Busby's world record for a goalkeeper of £23,500, his boyhood friend Jackie Blanchflower, and his wife Jean were waiting at Victoria Station, along with Matt Busby,

Jimmy Murphy and an army of Manchester pressmen.

'That was a nice gesture but typical of Matt because he knew I had played with Jackie as a schoolboy,' Gregg said. 'I got on great with the lads and I think they liked me. The most difficult ones to get to know were Bill Foulkes and Bobby Charlton, but I had played against Duncan, Tommy, and Roger and with Jackie so it wasn't as if I had never met them before.

'You see, running on to that pitch for Manchester United? You could not describe it. The most important man in football, though, is Joe Public for if they don't like you, that's it. But the United fans took to me, mainly because I carried on like a bloody idiot; I spent more time out of goals than in. The first game I nearly took Duncan's head off, but that was my way.'

Gregg arrived just in time to see Ray Wood sustain a broken cheekbone in the 1957 FA Cup Final. The two Manchester clubs fared badly with their goalkeepers at Wembley. City's Bert Trautmann famously suffered a broken neck in the final of 1956, Wood knocked cold 12 months later and Gregg himself was bundled over the line along with the ball, by Bolton's Nat Lofthouse three months after Munich. When Gregg appeared on Lofthouse's *This is Your Life* in April 1993 he admitted: 'I spent most of the rest of the match looking for a chance to even the score.'

Munich apart, the 50s were happy and fulfilling. 'The lads were typical of the time,' said Gregg. 'David Pegg was a real Jack the lad, a flashy dresser and an outgoing young fellow. Liam and Roger were two of the nicest men God ever put on the earth. Eddie Colman fancied himself as Frank Sinatra with his pork-pie hat. They were not angels you know. I remember in the dressing room when we played Luton Town and we got a draw when we should have won. Someone piped up: "Who was picking up the full-back?" and war broke out. It wasn't all sweetness and light. What typifies United to me is that at Doncaster, Monday, Tuesday, Wednesday and Thursday we would train. I got to Manchester United and we had Monday off and on the Tuesday morning a big coach would take us to The Meadows and we trained there. It was a doddle. Duncan, of course, wanted to go back in the afternoon.

'At Doncaster, drink was a taboo; when I got to Old Trafford there was a crate of beer against the kicking board in the dressing room. We spent all the time at Davyhulme golf course on the day before a game. We were all members. We would eat steak and egg or chicken. Drink sherry. Play cards, snooker. Then you would drive down Warwick Road in the bus with a big crowd, and stars in your eyes. Frankie goes to Hollywood, Harry goes to Hollywood.

'I stayed with Roger and Joy Byrne in Flixton for a time. Their dog pissed on the carpet in my bedroom and I was terrified they would think it was me.

'I remember the caper on the last night in Belgrade. There was a model Sputnik on rails going round the room, I can see it to this day, and I recall Mark Jones singing 'On Ilkley Moor Baht 'At'. I remember who went back to the hotel and who didn't. I remember Jackie Blanchflower hanging off a balcony pissed out of his mind. Then I remember in the hotel after the crash watching a flake at a time come down and the families arriving and having a bad time with the media. I remember a photographer in a long coat taking pictures.

'The saddest thing, apart from the carnage, was that I got sick and tired of going up and down in the hospital lift. I decided to walk up the stairs which were not well lit and before I got to top flight I could hear this terrible sobbing from round the corner and I looked round and Jimmy Murphy was sat halfway up the top flight crying his eyes out. I just turned and went back down.

'United, I have got to be proud I was there. There was the freshness of youth and it was all down to what Matt Busby created with a bunch of lads. He broke the mould and even before Duncan Edwards came in he went against everything football stood for at the time.'

Harry Gregg passed away on Sunday, 16 February 2020, at the age of 87.

Harry Gregg and friend relax on the glorious north coast of Co. Antrim.

DEFENDER OF THE REALM

West German Pierre Littbarski tries to escape the attentions of Italy's ruthless man-marker Claudio Gentile during the 1982 World Cup Final in Madrid. Littbarski was given special attention by the Libyan-born assassin (nickname Gaddafi) and never got a sniff (nor did Maradona of Argentina and Zico of Brazil in group matches) and Italy won 3–1.

Like many sports fans with nothing better to do I used to invent fantasy teams and always a team of Dirty Rotten Scoundrels. Like kids at a pantomime we need our villains.

As far as the real Dirty Rotten Scoundrels go there were the usual suspects: Harald Schumacher (the West German goalkeeper who assaulted Patrick Battiston of France in the 1982 World Cup), Harris (as above), Hunter, John Terry and, The Bastard's Bastard, Claudio Gentile of Juventus and Italy. Alongside 'Gaddafi' (he was born in Libya) our own 'Bite yer Legs' (Hunter), 'Chopper' (Harris) and 'Razor' (Ruddock) were clueless amateurs.

Gentile's demolitions of Argentina's Maradona, Brazil's Zico and, in the final, Pierre Littbarski of West Germany have passed into folklore and basically won Italy the 1982 World Cup. He was brilliant and the total master of the game's dark arts: trips, fingernails, kicks, shirt pulling, stamping, elbows in the face and bites (all missed by referees but available in the official film). As Gentile later retorted to a clueless reporter: 'Football is not for ballerinas.'

At Old Trafford fans tended to boo the likes of Chelsea's Ron Harris or Leeds United's Norman Hunter the

In 1982 the Football League selected 'the best brains in the business' to work out ways of making the game more entertaining.

There was a £5m publicity campaign, a first meeting, on 29 March at Highfield Road, Coventry, chaired by Jimmy Hill and big names: Bobby Charlton (closest), Hill (beard), Matt Busby (right of Hill) and FA secretary Graham Kelly. To Charlton's left is Graham Taylor (Watford) and others included Brian Clough (Nottingham Forest), Keith Burkinshaw (Spurs), Bertie Mee (formerly Arsenal), David Pleat (Luton Town), John Camkin (Coventry director), Ron Saunders (Birmingham City), John Lyall (West Ham) and John Bond (Man City).

One suggestion, and probably the most controversial at the time, was that those players committing 'professional fouls' should be sent off.

The concept had gained notoriety in the 1980 FA Cup Final when Arsenal's Willie Young deliberately fouled Paul Allen of West Ham when he had a clear run on goal. As the laws stood, referee George Courtney could only caution Young and award West Ham a free kick.

The intention of the Jimmy Hill think-tank was good and to call it 'a professional foul' was not a misnomer. There were players whose full-time 'profession' was to stop an opposition danger man . . . and at any cost. Some, like Claudio Gentile, were so 'professional' they almost always got away with it.'

moment they walked on the field, never mind at the opening whistle. I could actually have listed 100 naughty boys; Nobby Stiles wouldn't have been one of them.

To opposition fans he was a thug, the Old Trafford equivalent to Harris at Stamford Bridge or Hunter at Elland Road but that's a grave disservice for he was more skilled than sinful. Busby knew that, as did England manager Ramsey in 1966. To them Stiles was as crucial to a game plan as Charlton, or Moore, or Peters.

After the final group stage win over Mexico in 1966 Ramsey had threatened to resign if FIFA suspended Stiles for an alleged 'unsavoury' challenge. In the semi-final against Portugal the great Eusébio found himself shackled by a tiny Mancunian with bad eyesight and missing dentures.

Little wonder that Ramsey blew a fuse in the press conference later when a journalist asked him if he had told Stiles 'to deal with' Eusébio.

Nobby was never a man for pretentious motor cars à la Best (and Charlton and Busby at times). This was taken after a training session in March, 1965.

I approached Nobby Stiles for an interview in May 2002, hoping for memories of his early days at Old Trafford (1960 and just after Munich). He wasn't keen at first until I slipped in mentions of places and events common to both (north Manchester, the Harpurhey nursing home in which both were born, interviews I'd had with Albert Scanlon and Harry Gregg). A week after my call he had a heart attack and for that reason the interview never took place.

He has been battling Alzheimer's and vascular dementia for close to two decades now and, as happened with the family and the survivors of Munich, there has been little in the way of support within the game. To name one example the head of the PFA drew a salary of £2m in 2018 while PFA research into football head injury and degenerative brain disease was limited to £100k. Stiles felt it necessary to sell his medals in September 2010.

A year later he was diagnosed with prostate cancer and while recovering at Manchester's Christie Hospital he suf-

England manager Alf Ramsey welcomes his new caps at Stamford Bridge ahead of the British Championship 2–2 draw against Scotland at Wembley in April 1965. Left to right: Alf, Barry Bridges, Jackie Charlton and Nobby Stiles.

Nobby, aged 19, prepares for the 1961/2 season at Old Trafford. It was to be United's 60th season in the league, and their 17th consecutive season in the top division (they were relegated 10 years later). Back row: Shay Brennan, Bill Foulkes, Noel Cantwell, Harry Gregg, David Gaskell, Ronnie Cope (transferred to Luton a month later), Jimmy Nicholson. Front row: Albert Quixall, Stiles, Johnny Giles (Nobby's brother-in-law), Maurice Setters, David Herd, Dennis Viollet, Bobby Charlton.

Nobby Stiles and his skipper Bobby Moore organise England's defensive wall during the 1966 World Cup Final at Wembley. In the background: West German captain Uwe Seeler, the late Martin Peters and Bobby Charlton.

Nobby Stiles demonstrates one way of defending against Denis Law during a training session at Old Trafford in April 1967.

Two months after the World Cup win at Wembley in 1966 England's unlikely hero Nobby Stiles finds time for relaxation at home with two-year-old son John and wife Kay. John had five years at Leeds United.

fered a stroke. As I write this now it's one week after the death of World Cup winner Martin Peters after his long struggle with Alzheimer's. To counter this the FA and PFA have made promises and little else.

'Dad's illness hadn't even become obvious to us when the first promise of action came from the FA and PFA to look at the possible link,' said his son Rob recently. 'We are talking about the possibility that this is the football equivalent of industrial disease. The pleasure Dad brought to so many doesn't seem to count for anything now.'

I found some of the best words about Nobby in a Spanish website called colgadosporelfutbol (hung for football) and written by Alberto Llopis, a photographer

Nobby Stiles and Harry Gregg show remarkable restraint as they are taunted by Everton fans after the FA Cup semi-final defeat at Bolton on 23 April 1966. The only goal came from Colin Harvey, the White Pelé or part of the 'Holy Trinity' (Ball/Kendall/Harvey) as some Goodison fans liked to call him.

with Associated Press. The translation in the blog is not the best but, like some translations, more meaningful than the original: 'Dubbed the Nosferatu Stiles made history in World 1966 when his punches more than men, ankle and other parts rival prevented the rival in power almost did not want or play the ball.

'The late Eusebio gave up in the identity card in the game, both played in that World Cup. It was also there was a coincidence of life. Then it was another World Cup image Nobby Stiles hopping practising a dance their World Cup in one hand their denture in another. And it is that time in British football elbows were flying as fast as dentures and rare was not wearing a fake; hence the Nosferatu. Nobby Stiles, a player from another era, perhaps one of the toughest in history but also perhaps more noble than some of today.' More noble than some of today: I often wish I had written that.

Kay Stiles, Nobby and sons Robert, Peter and John at home in Middlesbrough in 1972. I can remember the Nobby stories that appeared almost daily in the *Gazette*, the daily paper in Teesside and the hilarious way they always described him: 'Boro star Stiles who also played for Manchester United'. Nobby made 57 appearances for Boro from 1971 to 1973.

Nobby takes on Spurs' Jimmy Greaves (to many the greatest English goal-scorer of all time) during a midweek First Division match at White Hart Lane in October 1968. The match ended 2–2, United's goals came from Pat Crerand and Denis Law and the home response from Alan Gilzean and Cliff Jones.

Either Nobby and Steve Kindon of Burnley are the best of pals or Nobby had been ordered to keep a grip of the player known in the game as 'The Runaway Wardrobe'. The match, at Turf Moor on 29 November 1969, ended in a 1–1 draw. Kindon is now one of the funniest after-dinner speakers around: 'I'm not saying Tommy Smith was hard but he was born on 5 April 1945 and a month later Germany surrendered.'

Nobby on his way to the service for Bobby Moore at Westminster Abbey on 28 June 1993.

Nobby Stiles with his eldest son John in March, 2012.

Those were the days, my friends. On 28 February 1972, Nobby Stiles was into his second year at Ayresome Park and, as often happens in sport, his old club arrived for an FA Cup 5th round replay. It had been 0-0 at Old Trafford but a penalty from Willie Morgan and goals from Best and Charlton gave the visitors a place in the quarter-final where they were beaten by Stoke. A disconsolate Stiles looks on as United celebrate the Best goal.

Stiles and his new boss Bobby Charlton pose for the Deepdale camera crew after Nobby had joined Preston as player-coach in August 1973. The smiles didn't last long. Charlton soon resigned (as did Nobby) but Stiles did take over as manager in 1977. Four years later Nobby was out too (Tommy Docherty taking over). For Nobby it came almost as a relief: 'I came to suspect I simply wasn't hard enough to be a manager,' he said.

WORLD WAR '66

I watched the final in the Seven Stars in Ketley, 300 yards from the offices of the *Shropshire Star* and close by the M5. As the match and the celebrations lasted most of an afternoon the memories are understandably vague (though I do remember seeing my first colour telly and almost being taken out by a juggernaut on my way back to work). England won and three Manchester United players had been involved so it was easy to be caught in the mythology of the event. It was a high point all round and it was only much later I started to catch the low points, of which there were many. I had seen old coverage of the infamous Battle of Santiago in the 1962 tournament and I had read Frank McGhee's report in the *Mirror*: 'The match is universally agreed by observers as

England captain Bobby Moore takes front row during
a photo shoot at Lilleshall on 9 June 1966. This was
the bulk of 27 chosen players (plus backroom staff)
ahead of the World Cup campaign minus manager
Alf Ramsey (never into photo sessions). Twelve days
later Ramsey cut five more. The luckless ones were
Bobby Tambling (Chelsea), John Byrne (West Ham),
Peter Thompson (Liverpool and only just visible
behind Moore's head), Gordon Milne (Liverpool) and
Keith Newton (Blackburn).

It's the summer of 1966 and Sean Connery, 007,
and *Magnificent Seven* star Yul Brynner meet seven
of the England World Cup squad during a visit to
Pinewood studio on (I kid you not) 7 July. The players
here are, front: Jimmy Greaves and Ian Callaghan.
Right to left, back: Martin Peters, Geoff Hurst,
Nobby Stiles and Bobby Moore. In the background is
goalkeeper Peter Bonetti.

This must be the only smile (in public at least) captured of Argentina captain Antonio Rattin during the 1966 World Cup tournament. His squad were based in Birmingham and this was taken four days before the opening Group 2 match against Spain. Argentina won 2–1 but things went downhill for Antonio and Co. His colleague Rafael Albrecht was sent off in the next match against West Germany and Rattin joined in him a walk of shame during the quarter-final against England.

the ugliest, most vicious and disgraceful in soccer history.'

Some of it was hilarious (the fighting was the standard of ten-year-old schoolboys) and everyone saw it as a one-off; that FIFA would make sure there would never be a repeat. Fat chance: the 1966 tournament was a collection of unsportsmanlike conduct, weak refereeing and shabby organisation.

Even FIFA's official film (*GOAL*) couldn't hide the evidence, despite the obvious attempts. Pelé, one of the few foreign player's I would have paid to watch, was kicked and badly injured in the first game, missed the second (which Brazil lost) and was relentlessly assaulted by Portugal's João Morais in the third. At one pointy Morais fouled Pelé once and, when he tried to get up, fouled him again even harder. Morais wasn't even cautioned, Pelé was carried off and he and the holders were out of the tournament.

After 65 minutes of the negative and totally unwatchable 0-0 draw between Argentina and West Germany at Villa Park Argentina's Rafael Albrecht was sent off for kneeing Wolfgang Weber (later to score the late equaliser against England) in the groin.

In the quarter-finals referee Jim Finney of St Helens had either missed (or ignored) Karl-Heinz Schnellinger of West Germany handling the ball on the line. Uruguay captain, Horacio Troche was then sent off for kicking Lothar Emmerich in the stomach and on his way out

I've always found this an oddity: resting after training on the Arsenal practice field at London Colney are ten of the players who played in the final against West Germany on 30 July. But no Geoff Hurst and the man he replaced, Jimmy Greaves, is seated front right!

> **It was alleged that the shoddy refereeing and the fact that all England matches were played at Wembley, amounted to match-fixing**

slapped West German captain Uwe Seeler in the face. Team-mate Héctor Silva followed him five minutes later after downing Helmut Haller and at the end Julio Cortés kicked Finney and was handed a six-match ban.

As all four quarter-finals started at the same time on the same day TV coverage was limited to highlights (apart from the England match) so we had to wait for FIFA's official

Nobby Stiles, with support from Alan Ball, gives Wolfgang Overath and Karl-Heinz Schnellinger the slip in the World Cup Final.

film to catch some of the atrocities that had invaded the 'Beautiful Game'. No problems for viewers of England's quarter-final at Wembley as it was all there in gory detail. The Argentina captain, Antonio Rattin, was sent off for dissent (by a West German referee who had no Spanish) after 35 minutes. It still took a very moderate England team another 46 minutes to score. Argentina were the better

Bobby Moore should have known better: it has been next to impossible to persuade a referee to change his mind and disallow a goal, particularly when you realise Herr Dienst is already on his way back to the centre circle. For Moore's team-mates it was absolute despair at the prospect of extra time. Left to right: George Cohen, Nobby Stiles, Martin Peters, Jack Charlton, Bobby Charlton and Gordon Banks. Helmut Haller, scorer of West Germany's first goal, looks too knackered to celebrate. I'd take a guess that the backside on the goal line belongs to Ray Wilson.

side, captain or not and, according to unofficial match facts committed 19 fouls to England's 33. As Rattin was later to put it, possibly justifiably: 'It was clear that the referee played with an England shirt on.'

There were a hundred conspiracy theories and they didn't all come from Latin America. Simon Burnton of *The Guardian* reported that on the day of England's semi-final against Portugal, the far-left Italian newspaper *Avanti!* wrote this headline: 'Quel brutto pasticcio dei Mondiali' (What an ugly mess of a World Cup).

It was alleged that the shoddy refereeing and the fact that all England matches were played at Wembley, amounted to match-fixing. Quite coincidentally West Germany beat the Soviet Union in the forgotten semi-final at Goodison Park after winger Igor Chislenko was sent off and Iosif Sabo injured himself trying to foul Franz Beckenbauer.

'Off the field,' said Burnton, 'trains for travelling fans were always late, matches started late, there were insufficient tickets for foreign journalists to go round, telephones in the press centres did not work properly. Telegrams to news desks around the world had been taking as long as three hours to arrive at the other end. Media accommodation in London, at university halls of residence a lengthy drive from the press centre, was "like a boarding school".'

The World Cup of 1966 was when I began to lose interest in the game. Many results seemed to be reliant

Sir Alf and his coaching staff begin one of the hardest jobs in sport: lifting the spirits of a team when they have just lost a goal in the dying minutes. Trainer Les Cocker is on the left, Ramsey centre and assistant manager Harold Shepherdson right. It took 43 years and some support from players and some politicians to persuade FIFA to give Cocker and Shepherdson commemorative medals. By then it was too late and in 2009 family members had to collect the medals on their behalf from PM Gordon Brown at Downing Street.

Some people are on the pitch . . . they think it's all over

on dubious officials and deliberate foul play. As has been noted Pelé, the greatest player who ever lived, was brutally and deliberately kicked out of the competition (no subs back then) by Portugal, who in their turn survived a 3–0 deficit thanks to North Korea losing their nerve and giving away two penalties.

England, by no means the best team in the tournament beat Argentina after the opposition captain got himself sent off. Geoff Hurst's equaliser in the final came from a free kick after Bobby Moore had been fouled and it was a foul by Jack Charlton that gave West Germany the chance to equalise and take the game into extra time.

Finally, did I mention Tofiq Bakhramov, the famous 'Russian linesman' who was actually from the Republic of Azerbaijan? There's a story that he was on his deathbed when he was asked about the Geoff Hurst goal that wasn't against West Germany and why he had awarded it. His one word reply was 'Stalingrad', which opens a whole new line in conspiracy theories.

. . . it is now

A smile (almost) from Sir Alf Ramsey as he joins up with his 1966 World Cup- winning side for a testimonial dinner at the Café Royal on 30 July 1974.

MORE DIRTY TRICKS

I first approached Manchester United plc in 2002 with an intention of writing a book about the Munich disaster. It didn't go well. The company had just achieved a record operating profit of £80.8m next to record earnings of £199.8m – thanks in the main to merchandising and branding (soda, lager, wine, cellular phone services and leisure complexes in Asia. Club representatives were happy to discuss this, but not events that in many ways had made all this affluence possible – the Busby Babes and the Munich air disaster. As assistant secretary Ken Ramsden told me within seconds of shaking hands in his office: 'We will simply not co-operate with anything that will damage the good name of the club.' Then, with what I would best describe as a sneer: 'Are you a fan who is trying to be a writer or a writer who is a fan?'

I told him the latter and knew then there would be no support from the club. I was told in no uncertain terms I would have to secure permission from the plc's chief executive to talk to employees, past and present, including Ramsden's mother and aunt (famously known as Omo and Daz) who were laundry ladies in the Busby Babes era. All my emails and telephone calls to the then-CEO, Peter Kenyon, went unanswered so in the end there were no interviews with Bobby Charlton (who graciously rang me in person to make his excuse), Bill Foulkes or Alex Ferguson (who turned me down via his secretary). Fortunately, former players, survivors and families no longer involved with the club agreed to talk.

It got nasty for a time. I had had long interviews with Harry Gregg and former Busby Babe John Doherty but just before publication a 'cease-and-desist or else' type letter arrived from a firm of Manchester solicitors (the same solicitors employed by Gordon Taylor's PFA. The claim was bizarre: not that I had 'misquoted' Gregg and Doherty (the usual allegation) but that they had never even met me.

This attempt to muddy the waters of a book critical of Manchester United plc fell apart when the solicitors

discovered that I had over eight hours of tape, that the meeting with Doherty had taken place in a crowded south Manchester hotel and that one of Gregg's daughters saw me arriving at the family home in Co. Antrim. Why did two old men put their names to this?

According to Doherty, who I had phoned just after the case was dropped, neither he nor Gregg not only knew anything about it but hadn't been approached by a firm of solicitors. Finally, a clue to Manchester United plc's devotion to filthy lucre in any form: within days of publication (uncensored) the book was on sale in the club's mucho moneymaking megastore.

I suppose I should thank the CEO at the time, Martin Edwards, for this piece of largesse, though the book was probably bought, like the megastore itself, players and stands, using other people's cash. The other odd thing about Martin Edwards is that he consistently proclaimed Manchester United as the 'love of his life', but consistently attempted to sell it: once to the fraudster Robert Maxwell in 1984, and five years later to Michael Knighton, a Yorkshire schoolmaster turned property developer.

Knighton ran out of backers almost as quickly as his famous ball-juggling act in front of a disbelieving Stretford

Another fine mess you got us into. Chairman Martin Edwards introduces 'new owner' Michael Knighton to the Press on 25 August 1989. Edwards, in an effort to explain why he became one of the most unpopular figures in the history of any club, claimed later: 'It was just that when we were approached we were to consider offers and options. They [shyster Robert Maxwell and Knighton] were the ones that probably didn't help my popularity.' After his Old Trafford deal fell through Knighton took over a less glamorous United, Carlisle, where he also served as manager. Like many owners he took criticism personally and for a time banned me and my newspaper from the ground.

The marvellous mind of Martin Edwards (right) seems to be elsewhere during the match against Norwich on 15 November 1986. His new manager, Alex Ferguson looks more engaged in this goalless draw at Carrow Road. It was Ferguson's second match in charge and his culling of the squad he had been left with wasn't far away.

End on 19 August 1989 and Edwards had to look elsewhere. He first backed BSkyB's (Murdoch) attempted takeover in September 1998, a bid beaten off by a combination of a fan backlash and the Monopolies and Mergers Commission. Still, Edwards continued to unload the shares in the 'love of his life', banking £41m by selling to friends of the horse-racing grandees John Magnier and J P McManus and another £21m to the Scottish property magnate, Harold Dobson. His fall, and final severance from the club, came in November 2002, when police questioned him over Peeping Tom allegations involving a woman guest at the Mottram Hall Hotel, Prestbury.

IF FANS REGARDED the Edwards as a family from hell, they ain't seen nothing yet. The Glazers – dad Malcolm, sons Avram, Joel, Kevin, Bryan, Edward and daughter Darcie – annexed the club in 2005 and immediately set about milking the cow.

As things stand today the club's net debt is some £391.3m and there's no sign of these slumlords, hedge fund wheeler-dealers (and Trump supporters) moving on. Apart from their love of other people's money Americans are supposed to be big on history (Independence, Civil War, World Series, Super Bowl, stuff like that) but the Glazers have never given a hoot about the history of the club they own. They didn't show for the 50th anniversary ceremonies of Munich, or the

60th ten years later and though that precipitated storms of fan outrage the club was better off without them.

The 60th anniversary wasn't the closure the club had obviously hoped for and that those pesky Mancs in Red would finally go away. They did make effort: complimentary match programmes with features on the team most consider the greatest ever, tributes to those who died and those who survived. There was a poster of the last line-up in Belgrade, black armbands for the players and the obligatory minute's silence. After that Manchester United plc could work on the concept of anniversaries only being significant if the year has 0 or a 5 at the end so minimal effort could be made until 2023 and the 65th anniversary.

The 'official' Old Trafford ceremony of 2019 was uneasily downbeat. Manager Ole Gunner Solkskjaer and former captain Bryan Robson were called in for the second year in succession and there was a curious debut for women's head coach Casey Stoney. The embarrassment was completed when the Sky film crew, whether deliberately or not, kept their cameras trained on a sign pointing the way to the nearest loo.

On the same day Bayern Munich, a club whose only real justification for a ceremony about an air crash involving a rival team was that it happened in its city and one of its hospitals saved a lot of lives, showed how it was done. It was an unforgettable occasion.

Chairman Karl-Heinz Rummenigge, supported by President Herbert Hainer, honorary president Uli Hoeness, Munich city counsellors and members of the Manchester Munich Memorial Foundation, laid a foundation stone at the crash site in Trudering. Rummenigge's moving speech will always be remembered, too: 'There is a great friendship between the two clubs and this has only deepened and strengthened over the years.' Not for the first time I wonder how Manchester United plc would have responded had a Lufthansa with Bayern Munich players on board crashed in Stretford?

Bayern Munich, a club whose only real justification for a ceremony was that the air crash happened in its city, showed how it was done. It was an unforgettable occasion

On 26 April 1958, the last day of the season (players got a break in those days) Sheffield Wednesday beat champions Wolverhampton Wanderers 2–1 in front of a full house at Hillsborough. Wednesday had just been relegated and long-term manager Eric Taylor was about to hand over to Harry Catterick. Catterick, one of the best wheeler-dealers in the business, almost immediately sold the club's Golden Boy to Manchester United. Here Albert Quixall, wearing the famous Owls colours for the last time, does battle with Gerry Harris of Wolves.

Quixall was 5ft 8ins tall (but at 11st plus bulky with it) and tend to keep his feet on the ground. Here he is, facing Burnley's centre-back John Talbot with Brian Miller (later to have two spells as manager at Turf Moor) charging in to help. Burnley always seemed to field a platoon of defensive heavyweights (keeper Adam Blacklaw weighed in at 15st) though it didn't h on 4 May 1963 as a Denis Law goal gave United, who had been flirting with relegation for the latter part of the season, a win.

S NEW AGAIN

With five of the Munich survivors (Gregg, Charlton, Foulkes, Viollet and Scanlon) capable of playing at a competitive level Manchester United managed to produce a remarkable 1958/59 season to finish as runners-up to Billy Wright's Wolverhampton Wanderers. Wright, who had recently married Joy of the Beverley Sisters, retired almost immediately . . . as did Jackie Blanchflower whose injuries at Munich had ensured he would never play again. As his wife Jean and two children were soon to discover the biggest battles lay ahead.

The season 1959/60 was a different matter. There were five defeats in the first ten games, including heavy losses to Spurs, Preston and Manchester City and a seventh place in the end. It was obvious Busby needed reinforcements, particularly in defence, but he stuck to the customs of '48 and '58: score more goals than the opposition (even if it meant giving away a few) and, above all, 'go out and enjoy it'.

United's goal differences said everything: 102 for, 80 against, one of the worst in the First Division with only Chelsea, Leeds, West Ham and Manchester City any worse. It was a season in which Busby thrashed around, moving players, sacking one or two, tearing things up and putting them down again and hoping they will eventually settle. There was a half-hearted attempt to persuade

Quixall chose a more secure business after he retired from football in the late '60s . . . running a scrapyard close to Old Trafford.

the new England full-back Jimmy Armfield away from Blackpool but Armfield was the definitive one-club man and Busby had to look elsewhere.

Instead he paid a record £45,000 for Albert Quixall of Sheffield Wednesday . . . a forward. It was baffling. Up front he could field Charlton, Viollet, Alex Dawson and Albert Scanlon (six goals including a hat-trick in his first ten games in 1959), none of whom had cost him a penny. The standard joke became: 'Matt must have picked the wrong Albert.'

Quixall had blond hair, (short shorts) and wonderful ball-playing skills to go with 66 league and cup goals, but the transfer bewildered even him (he signed without even knowing the size of the fee). The move and its aftermath were laced with the irony recurrent in sport.

Quixall was in the Wednesday side beaten 3–0 in the emotional FA Cup tie at Old Trafford in February 1958 and 12 months later was in the United side beaten 1–0 at home in the same round of the FA Cup by Wednesday.

The Owls immediately not only went back up to the First Division but finished above United in the following four seasons

Leeds boss Don Revie can't keep the smirk off his face as he leads Johnny Giles out of Old Trafford on 29 August 1963. He had just paid £33,000 for the Republic of Ireland superstar and Giles was about to pay back in spades. 'I am going to haunt him [Busby],' Giles had promised. And so he did.

Quixall, who remembered playing for and against Roger Byrne, Tommy Taylor, Duncan Edwards, David Pegg and Mark Jones at schoolboy, army and international level, was a member of United's FA Cup-winning side in 1963. He scored 56 goals in 184 games but went out of Busby's favour about the same time as Johnny Giles. He may also be remembered for 'Doing a Beckham' in a pre-season friendly against Bayern Munich in 1959, lobbing the goalkeeper from half way straight after kick-off . . . and then being sent off!

Busby, rather irrationally, was still waiting for another Duncan Edwards to bounce over the old ground's picket fence, march on to the field and lead him to the Promised Land. It turned out there had been one, almost as good, at Old Trafford for years ... and his name was Johnny Giles.

Ten out of ten for the photographer who captured Dennis Viollet, Bobby Charlton and Johnny Giles in full flight during training on 4 August 1960.

● Cinderella will come to the ball! Six-year-old Michelle Brennan reads her favourite fairy tale just after daddy Shay had been recalled to the Manchester United team in 1967.

Shay had a 13-year career at Old Trafford, though not always in the first team. The Manchester-born Republic of Ireland international (the first Irish international to qualify through parentage) scored twice in the emotionally charged FA Cup tie against Sheffield Wednesday on 19 February 1958, but struggled to hang on to a regular first-team place after that. Busby seemed to have problems finding the right combination of Foulkes, Ian Greaves, Joe Carolan or Ron Cope. Shay spent long periods in the reserves until, as Michelle might say, dreams do come true!

Shay was a member of the 1965 and 1967 championship squad and played a key role at Wembley '68. After moving to Ireland to take over as player-manager of Waterford United, he won two titles there and three more international caps.

He was 63 when he suffered a fatal heart attack while playing golf at the Tramore club on 9 June 2000. He is buried near there.

I RETURNED TO OLD Trafford on Monday, 7 October 2002. It was a small lifetime since the last visit on 19 February 1958 and how things had changed. I had wangled a free ticket and joined Roy Keane's despised corporate spectator brigade in the club's Platinum Lounge along with 60 or so current and potential sponsors, semi-semi-famous celebrities Angus 'Statto' Loughran and Derek 'Deggsy' Hatton . . . and the very-very famous Paddy Crerand.

Everton were beaten 3–0, despite a man-of-the-match display by their bald Danish midfielder Thomas Graveson (now living the high life in Las Vegas, I gather) and a cameo from a 17-year-old called Wayne Rooney. Two other things struck me about that night: a lack of passion almost funereal among home fans (dominant teams in any sport tend to make fans quite blasé, arrogant even) and an introduction to Paddy Crerand.

Like some Glaswegians I knew there was a smiley air of menace about Crerand and instead of shaking hands he squeezed an arm so tight it hurt. Then, moving in close, he hissed: 'Don't I know you from somewhere?'

A day later, still preening myself and looking for someone, anyone, to tell that I had actually met Paddy Crerand I rang a friend close to the club and broke my news, to which he replied: 'Paddy always does that. It's part of his corporate hospitality routine.

'Now you'll be going round telling everyone you met Paddy Crerand in United's Platinum Lounge, what a great night it was and how you'd like to go back . . . and actually pay next time.'

One of the six goals Brennan scored in 13 years with United was this one during a 3–0 win over Nottingham Forest (managed by Old Trafford legend Johnny Carey) on 23 March 1968. Forest goalkeeper Brian Williamson is beaten; George Best looks on. The other goals came from David Herd and Shay's fellow full-back, the teenager Francis Burns.

Never a man to forget his roots, Gorbals-born Paddy Crerand and Celtic team-mate Charlie Gallagher mix it with Glasgow street kids in 1960. Gallagher, a member of the Lisbon Lions squad of 1967 could have represented Scotland but, with a similar Irish parentage to his cousin Paddy, chose the Republic of Ireland. Crerand signed for Manchester United in 1963. Memorable for his devastating passing skills (and the speed of an Easter Island statue) he played close to 400 games for Manchester United and scored 15 goals.

Two months before his finest hour at Wembley, Brennan was already planning for the future. In partnership with former team-mate Bobby English and with professional shop opener Denis Law in support, he opened a carpet showroom on the edge of Manchester city centre.

Bobby Charlton shows Dennis Viollet, Shay and Bill Foulkes how it's done during a ten-pin bowling session at Cheetham Hill in September 1961. Ten-pin bowling was the new craze in the UK at the time and the Cheetham Hill alley (formerly the Odeon cinema) had only just been opened. Like a lot of trends it didn't last long; the old building was demolished in 1971 and is now a B&Q.

Within months of arriving in Manchester in 1963 Crerand was holding the FA Cup after United had beaten Leicester 3–1 at Wembley. Left to right: Tony Dunn, David Gaskell, Bobby Charlton, captain Noel Cantwell, Crerand, Albert Quixall, David Herd, Johnny Giles and Maurice Setters.

◄ It's a boy! Mother Noreen and dad Paddy are delighted with the sleepy new arrival, Patrick John Crerand.

► It's a girl! A bonny lass named Lorraine, born in April 1967.

It was difficult, in the 60s at least, to find a Manchester United player who did NOT play golf. Here are Denis Law, Paddy and Maurice Setters starting a round at Fairhaven near Lytham St Annes on 16 November 1964. Bill Foulkes was said to be the Old Trafford Master, though, by all accounts, never in the class of Dwight Yorke (handicap +3)!

Introductions all round for the tallest new boy in history as Ian Ure arrives from Arsenal (via Dundee) in August 1969. The blond giant had been signed as a replacement for the 37-year-old Bill Foulkes, whose distinguished career was coming to an end after 11 remarkable years. Foulkes is on the left, next to George Best, Paddy Crerand, John Fitzpatrick, Ure, Willie Morgan, Denis Law and manager Wilf McGuiness.

Stein and Shankly indulge some polite arm wrestling at Glasgow airport ahead of Liverpool's meeting with Celtic in the European Cup Winners' cup match in April 1966. Liverpool lost this first leg at Parkhead by a goal to nil, but prevailed at Anfield in the return (thanks to a disallowed goal by Celtic's Bobby Lennox).

A sports quiz at Pontins, Blackpool, in May 1968 starring former managerial rivals, a grinning Joe Mercer, a beaming Tom Finney and a smiling (or should it be snarling?) Bill Shankly. Shankly may have been born without a sense of humour (cracking old jokes and being rude about foreigners does not imply a sense of humour) but there was no arguing with his record of 15 years at Anfield: transforming a second-rate club, stuck in the lower ranks of the Second Division, to the winning of that title, then three First Division titles, two FA Cups and a Uefa Cup.

● Scotland manager Jock Stein famously hated smoking and drinking ('bad habits for wee fittballers') and also disliked beards and taches.

Here he checks to make sure Paddy Crerand had got the message before a flight to Poland for a World Cup qualifier (a 1–1 draw in Chorzów) on 23 May 1965. Billy McNeill is there as back-up. Stein could be something of a mini-tyrant and it always struck me as odd that three of the most revered Scottish managers of working-class mining stock – Stein, Busby and Shankly – acted this way once they got power. These alleged 'socialists' liked to keep players' wages at a minimum and all three had unpleasant sides, notably Shankly. In the 60s Liverpool had arranged a game at Bury's Gigg Lane for striker Ian St John, who was recovering from injury. The northern press were out in force: John Keith (*Express*), Bob Russell (*Mirror*), Denis Lowe (*Telegraph* and BBC) plus me (*Weekly News*, my first job). The match was played 'behind closed doors' so we had to wait in the cold for two hours in the hope of getting a usable 'quote'.

There were usually good relationships between sports writers and managers and players in those days but Shankly delighted in making life as hard as possible. 'Nae comment,' said the great man in that lovable way of his as he marched out, followed by a rather sheepish St John. Lowe was outraged. He did work for the BBC and the *Telegraph*, but was officially a freelance with income dependant on 'quotes' (as Shankly was well aware) and he replied: 'Fuck you then.'

Any Liverpool fan who thinks this is journalistic sour grapes should read 'The Saint' in his eponymous autobiography and the section about his final days at Anfield: 'Bill Shankly dropped me without saying a word, without even meeting my eyes.'

Patrick Timothy Crerand prepares for battle in 1970.

● Noel Eucharia Cornelius Cantwell leads his troops out to face Blackpool at Old Trafford on 23 February 1963.

Behind the captain are David Herd (the United scorer in the 1–1 draw), Harry Gregg and Johnny Giles. Noel Cantwell has never really been given the credit for his work at Old Trafford from the years he joined from West Ham in 1960 to 1967, the year he retired.

Intelligent, charming and cultured, the obits said of him, but football scribe Eamonn Dunphy also hinted that his fellow Irishman could be devastatingly blunt at times. 'Doesn't anybody actually talk, or even think, about the game here?' he had asked just after his arrival at Old Trafford. 'Why isn't training organised? Why don't we ever see Busby? Just a bit of running, head tennis, then round the back for a free-for-all kick about . . . Then, pre-match, Busby's simplistic "enjoy it lads and just give it to a red shirt". Give it to a fuckin' red shirt! You don't need a manager for that. How do you find a red shirt to pass to if you haven't planned it, worked on it, thought about it and talked about it?' Cantwell was 73 when he died in 2005.

Noel hangs on tight to the FA Cup at St Pancras station after the win over Leicester at Wembley in May 1963.

United's regular left-back in the '60s was the speedy Tony Dunne, a Dubliner who had joined around the same time as Cantwell in 1960 and who spent 13 years at Old Trafford without anyone really noticing him, so self-effacing was he. Here he is lending support to Nobby Stiles and Matt Busby after an FA hearing at the Midland Hotel, Derby, on 21 November 1966. Nobby had been fined and severely censored.

Cantwell pictured at home with son Robert in October 1966.

Footballers aren't generally known for their intelligence but several have contradicted that stereotype down the years: Socrates of Brazil (doctor of medicine and philosophy and smoker of exotica), Steve Heighway of Liverpool (economics), Graeme Le Saux of Chelsea (*Guardian* reader) and Manchester United's Alan Gowling. While making 87 appearances for the club between 1967 and 1972 Gowling found the time to earn a degree in economics at Manchester University. His nickname at Old Trafford, it goes without saying, was Bamber (as in Gascoigne).

● John Fitzpatrick kisses wife Barbara goodbye before setting off to an FA disciplinary committee meeting at Derby in November 1969.

The beaks, quite irrationally, banned him for eight matches on the grounds that he had logged up too many yellow cards (on the same day Derek Doogan of Wolves got eight matches for a sending-off).

Fitzpatrick was what fans would call a feisty wee character (à la Nobby Stiles) without noticing other abilities. Rivals often set out to provoke him, notably

AC Milan in the European Cup semi-final first leg in 1969. He retaliated to a spit, was sent off and, it being Milan, needed a police escort to the changing room.

But most of the memories are good: FA Youth Cup medal with Best, Aston and Sadler in 1964 (United wouldn't win it for another 28 years) and important roles in the European Cup campaign of 1968 (though he wasn't picked for the final).

After retirement he opened a wine import business in his home city of Aberdeen.

▲ A manager's philosophy: find an
on-form rival and go out and buy him.
Here's David Herd in an Arsenal jersey
(99 goals from 166 matches) in October
1959 taking on Ron Cope. Two years later
Busby (still fixated on his search for a
super-striker) paid £40,000 for him.
Herd, a Lanc, would probably have played
in the European Cup Final at Wembley in
1968, had he not broken his leg the year
before. The accident limited his first-team
opportunities from then on.

▶ Manchester United faced t
amateurs Hibernians of Malt
in the European Cup first rou
first leg at Old Trafford on 2(
September 1967. Here David
Sadler headed one of his two
goals in the 4–0 victory . . . b
it was quite disconcerting fo
many when a full-strength
United were held to a 0–0 dr
in the return.

Might as well be spring: David Sadler and fiancée Christine Halliday, a freelance artist of Talbot Road, pose for the cameras in Stretford Park. This was taken a month ahead of their wedding on 23 June 1968.

WILL THAT D

FOR NOW?

It was 6 May 1967, the penultimate game of the season, and Manchester United had produced one of their greatest performances for a long time to demolish West Ham 6–1 at Upton Park (Law 2, Best, Charlton, Crerand and Foulkes). But the days of wine and roses would soon be over. There was an FA Cup third round defeat by Spurs at the beginning of 1968 and home defeats to West Brom (6–3) and a 2–1 loss to Sunderland on the last day of the season handed the title to Manchester City. There was only one title left for Busby.

As Scottish friends won't cease to remind me, Manchester United wasn't the first British team to win the European Cup. A Celtic team, all bar one born within ten miles of Parkhead, Glasgow, beat Inter Milan 2–1 in Lisbon 12 months previously. It would take a curmudgeon to argue that this wasn't the greater triumph, particularly when knowing that six of the Busby team were not born within 100 miles of Manchester. We can call them, quite justifiably, the 'first English' side but it doesn't carry the same clout as 'first British'.

The 1968 final was also scheduled for Wembley, a second home for some of Busby's squad, notably Charlton and Stiles.

Hibernian (not the Edinburgh version but a Malta side coached by a Valetta priest) were United's first opponents (in 1967 Celtic drew FC Zürich, who had reached the European Cup semi-finals three years previously). The Maltese duly lost 4–0 at Old Trafford, but then held United to a 0-0 draw in Valetta. This was another potent clue that time was running out for Busby and his ageing team. They beat Górnik Zabrze in the quarter-final and were through to their fourth European Cup semi-final where they faced an equally long-toothed Real Madrid side; captain Francisco Gento, so often the scourge of United in the past was 35 years old.

◄The team board a plane at Ringway for Madrid and the semi-final second leg on 14 May 1968.

▲United captain Denis Law and opposite number Francisco Gento lead their teams out in the first leg of the European Cup semi-final at Old Trafford on 24 April 1968.

United went to Madrid with a slender 1–0 lead (Best) on 15 May and Real quickly turned the screw. By half-time they were 3–1 ahead on aggregate and the writing seemed to be on the wall. Madrid lost it, having forgotten that defenders are allowed to score goals, too. David Sadler, pictured here as he celebrates his goal, took United into touching distance and fellow defender Bill Foulkes finished the job. It was the first time anyone could ever recall Foulkes venturing past the halfway line.

Hail the unlikely hero: trainer
Jack Crompton hugs match
winner Bill Foulkes as Madrid
goes wild.

▶Norma Charlton (now Lady Norma) waves for the cameras as she climbs aboard the club train at Manchester Piccadilly station on 28 May 1968. Norma and other wives and girlfriends were en route to London and Wembley Stadium for the European Cup Final. A day later husband Bobby scored two goals in the 4–1 win over Benfica. Norma and Bobby were married in 1961, one year ahead of Denis and Diana Law. Golden days indeed!

▲Was this Busby's dress rehearsal for the final? This was taken on the pitch at Old Trafford two days before the team travelled down to London. It looks uncannily similar to extra time at Wembley when Busby, famously, marched on to the side of the pitch and cajoled his troops to greater effort.

● Ever the gentleman, Eusébio congratulates two-goal hero Bobby Charlton after the World Cup semi-final win over Portugal at Wembley on 27 July 1966. Two years later Eusébio was congratulating another United player, goalkeeper Alex Stepney, after a miraculous save in the European Cup Final.

Eusébio died in 2014 and Charlton again was asked for a tribute, something he has become quite accomplished at: 'Without doubt, Eusébio was one of the finest players I ever had the privilege to play against. Not only that, he was a true sportsman. I met him on numerous occasions after our playing careers had finished and he always represented both his club and his country in exemplary fashion. I feel proud to have been both an opponent and friend and am saddened to hear of his passing.'

The Portuguese champions, Benfica, were United's final opponents at Wembley and again the omens were better than the form. A Best-led United had dismantled the same opposition 5-1 in Lisbon's Stadium of Light in 1966 and Stiles, as he had demonstrated in the World Cup semi-final against Portugal in the same year, seemed to have the number of the Benfica danger man, Eusébio. Charlton had also enjoyed one of his best games for England against the Portuguese in 1966, scoring the two goals that took England into the World Cup Final. But United still made heavy work of Benfica two years later. Charlton's first goal on 53 minutes should have sufficed, but they conceded a needless equaliser when the gangling centre-forward Jose Torres,

engaged in an often-comical duel with Foulkes, nodded down a cross for Jaime Graca to lash past Alex Stepney. The goalkeeper's stupendous stop from Eusébio close to full time had, like most great saves, an element of fortune about it and the match winner, in the end, turned out to be the unsung and unheralded left-wing John Aston, who ran the Portuguese ragged in extra time.

Charlton leaps into the air in celebration after heading the first goal.

Charlton once claimed that he never wept when he lost a match but almost always when he won. Here Bill Foulkes helps the emotional Charlton off the field at Wembley on 29 May 1968.

Brian Kidd, Bobby Charlton,
Paddy Crerand and (soon to be
Sir) Matt Busby on the night the
dream came true.

Alex Stepney saves the day again, this time hanging on to the European Cup trophy from George Best. They had just arrived back at Old Trafford from Wembley in 1968.

● Surrey-born Alex Stepney won only one England cap (a 3-1 defeat by Sweden in 1969) but Old Trafford fans would be happy to hand him a hundred medals after his save against Eusébio in 1968.

It turned out much later that Stepney had studied United's 5-1 win in Lisbon in 1966 (the year he joined Manchester United from Chelsea) and Eusébio in particular.

It was 1-1 at Wembley two years later and he remembers: 'All of this gave me a chance regarding the save in the European Cup Final, towards the end when it was 1-1. Was I thinking: "It's near the end and I need to keep United in the Cup"? Well, you're lost in the moment.

'The Wembley turf in those days was slow, lush – when the ball was played through I thought it was probably a 55-45 ball for me but it slowed up and Eusébio was on to it. But this gave me the chance to stand up against him.

'I knew he wanted to burst the back of the net because that's the way he scored most of his goals. So that helped me.

'After making the save I didn't quite follow what happened. I saw it on telly afterwards and what had happened was that Eusébio had stood there applauding. Well, that's the kind of man he was; he was a gentleman.'

▲ And what a gentleman he was as he demonstrated at the banquet at the Royal Garden Hotel in Kensington after England's World Cup win in July 1966. Hat-trick hero Geoff Hurst looks on as Eusébio meets Mrs Hurst and cup.

A tender farewell from Alex Stepney to fellow goal tender Gordon Banks at the Stoke Minster funeral on 4 March 2019.

● John Aston Snr with Wembley man of the match John Jnr on the train back to Manchester. Paddy Crerand once said of John's performance at Wembley that 'he left that guy with twisted brains'; hard to better that as the description of a winger dominating a full-back.

Benfica made the same mistake as Real Madrid had in Madrid two weeks previously when David Sadler and, remarkably Bill Foulkes, found holes in a defence too busy looking for Best.

Benfica's Brazilian manager Otto Gloria admitted as much later: 'I laid plans for coping with Best and Charlton and the other stars but nobody warned me about this boy Aston.'

Aston galloped past Adolfo (nickname The Locomotive) and down Benfica's right flank at will. He played 155 times for United between 1965 and 1972 – scoring 25 goals and after retirement in 1980 opened a pet shop in Stalybridge.

'It was the family business,' he said. 'I started by helping out in the afternoons and then ended up running it. Aston Snr, capped 17 times for England and a wing-half with the post-war Busby side that won the FA Cup and two league titles, was also a youth coach at Old Trafford.

There's a plaque named for him at Ravensbury Community School in Tartan Street, Clayton, Greater Manchester, John Snr's first school from 1926 to 1935

Cheers! Brian Kidd and Johnny Aston raise a toast to the boss on the way back home. Kidd also has something named after him (local communities do this sort of thing far better than football clubs); a park and children's play area in Collyhurst, also famous as the birthplace of Les Dawson, Nobby Stiles and Stan Bowles, among others.

The site – next to St George's Community Centre on Bothwell Road – is opposite the house where Brian was brought up on Rome Road. Kidd made more than 200 first-team appearances for United, scoring more than 50 goals, before a move to Arsenal in 1974.

His coaching career began with the Old Trafford youth team before being appointed assistant manager under Alex Ferguson from 1991 to 1998.

He is now part of Pep Guardiola's coaching team at Maine Road (sorry, still find it hard to write the Etihad Stadium). 'I've been lucky to have had a long association with both clubs,' said Kidd recently, 'United and City, as a player and a coach and enjoyed great moments with both. I feel very privileged to have had that honour during my lifetime. And as a local lad it means a lot to me.'

Brian Kidd does a Denis Law and goes all blue in December 2009. Kidd was to assist new manager Roberto Mancini who had just taken over after the sacking of Mark Hughes. Mancini, the current manager of Italy, lasted four years at Maine Road, but Kidd has displayed remarkable longevity since, outlasting Manuel Pellegrini and (possibly) Pep Guardiola.

W hen Manchester United did finally win the European Cup on that desperately hot and humid 29 May night in London, they had come to the end of a long and painful journey.

'Busby ends his quest for the Holy Grail' said the large headline in the *Manchester Evening News* and for once the hyperbole and poetic licence was justified, for it had been an Arthurian quest of fabulous proportions over 16 years. When the whistle blew at Wembley to end a technically mediocre match distinguished by the drama of extra time and two symbolic goals from Charlton himself, Busby walked on and headed straight for his captain. Their embrace told everything of the dramas they had shared, of the suffering, the frustration and the undoubted relief of that final fulfilment.

That European Cup victory came not a moment too soon. Charlton was 31 by then and had won everything worth winning, including a World Cup. Busby was close to 60, though suddenly looking much older. As were his players.

This, to many, was like the last day of the Roman Empire with the emperor (Busby) about to abdicate and Vandals (Manchester City) preparing to sack their city. There was little to celebrate for some time as the conquering heroes parade the trophy in front of thousands of fans en route to the town hall.

United and trophy meet the press at Old Trafford.

It was to be another 31 years before United got hands on the trophy again. After Wembley the only question left was, where now? King Arthur had his Holy Grail, a knighthood, the promise of some sort of sinecure at Old Trafford when he did go and a grown-up family.

His son, Sandy, has few doubts, either, that his father was losing his appetite for the day-to-day demands of football management. 'Dad, like all good managers had always had a very clear vision of what was good for the club. But sen-

The press turned up in force for Busby's first retirement on Tuesday, 14 January 1969. He handed the duties to Wilf McGuinness but stayed on as a director, a kiss of death for aspiring managers. McGuiness was duly sacked in December 1970, so the press had to turn out in force again to hear that Busby was taking over again. The job went to Frank O'Farrell in June 1971 (though by all accounts Busby had suggested Jock Stein or Don Revie, both of whom were wise enough to refuse).

timent came in in 1968 with that ageing team. He knew in his heart of hearts that it was time to start dismantling it and start building again. But at that stage of life, 60, he simply hadn't the heart or ruthlessness to ship Bobby and Bill Foulkes out to other clubs.

'George [Best] was always complaining that he was carrying an ageing team. Dad's decision to retire was because he no longer had the heart or ruthlessness to do what was needed to be done.'

● Smoke gets in your eyes … It's 15 August 1972 and Manchester United manager Frank O'Farrell is four months away from the sack as his side go down 2–0 against Liverpool at Anfield. The choppers in chief are Matt Busby, fag in hand, and chairman Louis Edwards, fag in mouth.

The image of Matt Busby remains that of a kindly grandfather who called his charges 'son' and preferred Jimmy Murphy to play the bad cop. In private Busby could be as ruthless as any and that includes Alex Ferguson.

Busby never went as far as the hairdryer treatment but, according to Frank O'Farrell, could be quite devious. He wasn't really the nice guy people saw in public.

As he was to reveal in a remarkable and telling interview years after his brief spell at Old Trafford in 1971 O'Farrell had first met Busby privately where he was informed why and how he had been chosen.

Busby said he wanted to step back from managing the club and, according to Farrell: 'The team had been together too long, some players were getting old and the team needed to be rebuilt.

'He said it was a five–year job and that he wanted me to take it on. I asked him what the terms of the contract would be. He said, "so many thousand bonus if you win the league, so many thousand if you win the cup, so many thousand for the European Cup and so on and a basic pay of £12,000." I said I'd think about it over the weekend, talk to my chairman at Leicester, and get back to him on Monday.

'I then arranged to meet Matt Busby and the chairman Louis Edwards to discuss the matter again. We were to meet in a hotel but Busby wasn't happy with that so I drove out to the country, found a lane where we parked and I sat in Louis Edwards' Rolls Royce to discuss the matter with them. I asked Matt would he repeat the terms again and he said "so many thousand for the league and so on …" and he finished with £12,000 your wages.

'At that point Louis Edwards interrupted and said: "No Matt you're wrong, it's £15,000." Of course I knew I was in trouble at that point.' When he did get to Old Trafford Busby showed him a new office they were building down the hall from the one Matt had always used and where he intended to stay. 'I told him that this wouldn't do. People would think that he was still the manager. He reluctantly agreed to move out of the office.'

O'Farrell wanted other changes. 'Manchester United was a difficult team,' he said. 'They had a funny attitude to tactics. If they score four, we'll score five was their attitude. That was all very well when they were 24 or 25, now the team was in its early 30s. George Best was carrying the team but he would go missing. Nobody knew if he was going to turn up. Denis Law was another peculiar person. If he wasn't playing he wasn't even interested in watching the game.'

When he dared drop Bobby Charlton (for three matches) O'Farrell could guess what was coming next.

After his sacking and the appointment of Tommy Docherty, who almost immediately led them into the Second Division, the club refused to honour O'Farrell's contract.

He started legal proceedings and had to go on the dole while waiting for the case to be heard. United agreed to settle in the end but it left O'Farrell, who

celebrated his 92nd birthday in October 2019, bitter about United and Busby in particular.

He told Raidió Teilifís Éireann: 'The club has a great reputation. But the people I was dealing with at that time weren't very nice people. And they were vindictive, punitive, and nasty people. Matt Busby was one of the worst of them. I have a very poor opinion of Matt Busby. I'm not taking away what he's achieved as a manager, but as a person, he doesn't come out on top of my list.'

THE DARK KNIGHTS

D avid Miller, for six decades a major league sports writer with the old *Daily Express* and *The Times* (and still going strong) has never bought into the Ferguson myth and made a brief appearance in social media the day Ferguson retired in 2013.

'Alex Ferguson,' he twittered, 'superb manager, shame he didn't behave more like Matt Busby, truly a Knight of the Realm.'

Miller wrote a biography of Busby (*Father of Football*, foreword by Bobby Charlton) so he may be a tad biased, but he was certainly wrong about one thing: Ferguson behaved just like Matt Busby.

There's a what may be described as a eulogy to

Alex Ferguson shows off
his UEFA Cup Winners'
Cup trophy in May
1991 after United had
beaten Barcelona 2–1 in
Rotterdam. It was his
first European title at
Old Trafford and though
it looks rather lame
alongside Matt Busby's
European Cup gong the
trophies flowed after this.
In a perverse sort of way
Ferguson (as did Busby)
contributed to the club's
falls from grace. As when
he left Aberdeen, no one
was able to fill his boots at
Old Trafford.

Ferguson in another Netflix documentary (*Sir Alex Ferguson's Secret of Success*) also starring some very rich friends (Lord Sugar, venture capitalist Sir Michael Moritz, a lady from Harvard Business School and Tony Blair) but little about his 'unique management skills'. There were no mentions of the post-war teams, the Busby Babes, Munich and the European Cup win at Wembley in 1968.

There were quotes from a few football types – Cristiano Ronaldo, Jose Mourinho, Ryan Giggs and Rio Ferdinand – and all of them echoing the opinions of Busby I had heard 60 years previously.

Ferdinand, the Dennis Viollet of his day, feigned astonishment that Ferguson had discovered his fondness for the Manchester nightlife and had warned him off it.

I remembered a long interview with Sandy Busby (Matt's late son): 'Dad always knew where a player had been. A lot of them forgot that Manchester is a village in many ways and it was hard to hide anywhere. There were always spies and plenty of tittle-tattle.'

Cristiano Ronaldo was also amazed that 'the boss knew everyone's name' and I remembered Busby remembering my name though we had met twice, and both times among a crowd of other reporters.

Ferguson, it's claimed in the Netflix documentary, 'set up a unique scouting system' as if this had just been invented and which begs the obvious question: Where did Busby and Murphy find Duncan Edwards, Bobby Charlton and Liam Whelan to name but three?

Ferguson himself was asked (by political commentator Nick Robinson) why he tolerated Eric Cantona and his kung fu assault on a Crystal Palace fan in 1995 but got rid of the likes of Paul McGrath, Roy Keane and seven or eight others for varying reasons?

Ferguson hedged that one but I could have told Robinson this: Without Cantona Ferguson wouldn't have won his second double in 1997 . . . in the same way that Manchester United wouldn't have won the European Cup in 1968 without George Best. Busby didn't hesitate in getting rid of Johnny Morris, Charlie Mitten, Dennis Viollet and Johnny Giles. Don't believe the fairy tale about Busby (and that means Murphy) 'missing the potential' of Giles, a player who had won a Republic of Ireland cap at 18 and four years had been a regular first-teamer at Old Trafford. Even in those days Giles tended to speak his mind and Busby would never tolerate that.

Like Ferguson and his choice of David Moyes later Busby wasn't very good at choosing a successor when the time came to retire.

Wilf McGuinness, who lasted 18 months, was a disaster and then it was decided he had made a mistake by bringing in Frank O'Farrell. The Irishman was treated abysmally during his short spell at Old Trafford.

There were some obvious differences between the two Scots: Ferguson didn't begin his United career in the middle of a south Manchester bomb site and didn't have to recover from the physical and mental scars that nearly killed Busby at Munich (Ferguson's 2018 brain haemorrhage was long after retirement).

Busby would never have allowed himself to become involved in an unseemly row over the ownership of a race horse, Rock of Gibraltar, and the negative press that went with it.

Finally, the most meaningful difference: Busby had Murphy as a right-hand man for 25 years, Ferguson used seven: Archie Knox 1986–91, Brian Kidd 1991–98, Steve McLaren 1999–2001, Jimmy Ryan 2001–02, Carlos Queiroz 2002–03 and 2004–08, Walter Smith 2004 and Mike Phelan 2008–13.

> **Like Ferguson and his choice of David Moyes later Busby wasn't very good at choosing a successor when the time came to retire**

The last farewell and a silent vigil for Sir Matt
Busby outside Old Trafford on 20 January 1994

ALL GLORY

You could fill a large bookshelf with biographies of Busby, Stein and Shankly, the three Scots from mining stock who once dominated British football. There were to be no happy endings for two of the 'Three Kings', as one writer titled them. Stein was 62 when he died of a heart attack at the end of a World Cup qualifying match at Ninian Park, Cardiff, on 10 September 1985. It was a very public departure. A TV crew and photographers were there to catch his final minutes and dozens of reporters, there to cover the match, were suddenly forced into hasty re-writes.

'I watched yards away as a night of joy ended in tragedy,' said Rodger Baillie in the Scottish Sun, cleverly making his job that night as important as the death of Stein. It turned ugly at times. Scottish fans sent death threats to some of the photographers, having decided that Stein had lost his temper when the snappers got too close at the final whistle and this had precipitated the heart attack.

Shankly was 68 when he had died of a heart attack four years previously. Both were teetotal and non-smokers and without trying to score a point, Busby, a devotee of Scotch, a pipe and Rothmans, survived well into his 80s, outlasting his two friends by some distance.

The media coverage of the deaths of the three followed a standard course: factual obituaries, praise from family, friends, contemporaries and non-critical memoirs. It didn't take long, however, before some of

IS FLEETING

those contemporaries decided this might be a good time to pay off some old scores: John 'Yogi' Hughes on his former Celtic boss Stein ('intimidating, inhumane, and corrupt'), Ian St John on Shankly (see page 195) and Frank O'Farrell on Busby (see page 228) to name but three.

Shankly often liked to draw a comparison between his retirement and that of Busby mainly because Busby kept a role in the running of the club and Shankly, for various reasons, was pushed into the wilderness. Unlike Busby, Shankly was never offered a seat on the club board and after the directors called his bluff (Shankly was a serial retiree-threatener) and let him go, there was little in the way of outrage from fans who had once called him the messiah.

There is an obvious reason for this: there had been a line of lieutenants who had been groomed to take his place and Bob Paisley – followed by Joe Fagan – provided a better win/loss ratio than their departed leader. For the majority of fans at any club, that would do.

According to James Corbett, writing in The Observer in 2009, 'by the time of his death Shankly was a tragic figure, the forgotten architect of Liverpool's footballing supremacy.' Almost from the day he had announced his 1974 retirement 'Shankly knew it was the worst mistake of his life and the game had easily carried on without him'. In the end he was banned from their training ground at Melwood which, to a man like Shankly, was as painful as a punch in the stomach.

It would be hard (even dangerous) for the Old Trafford board to treat Busby with such ignominy, though chairman Louis Edwards did his best, reneging on a promise of a place on the board for Matt's son Sandy and bringing in his own boy, Martin, instead. Sandy was to spend 20 years managing the club gift shop.

After his official retirement in 1969, Busby had been loaded with personal rewards: a knighthood, a place on the board, an (unnecessary) testimonial in 1991 and a second appearance on This Is Your Life (the third if you count the one masquerading as Charlton's appearance in 1969). But it was never enough.

Sandy, long after Busby's death, told me

he had always thought that when his father announced 'he was going to call it a day' he should have meant it literally. He could have escaped with Lady Jean to the family holiday home at Cleveleys on the Fylde Coast and spent his final years in peace.

'He had lost his appetite for the demands of management,' said Sandy. However he also said: 'But he still wanted to be involved.'

Which he did. Unlike Stein and Shankly, the archetypal Grumpy Old Men, it was always hard to dislike Busby. He had the mind of a successful politician: the right time to smile or frown, a gift for putting his fellow man at ease and always able to put names to faces. Even when quite young, he was seen as an avuncular figure, the father of football as some liked to call him. The ruthlessness was hidden well away from the public.

He certainly had enemies. His treatment of a number of players, notably some of the Munich survivors, was disgraceful and few will forgive him for his interference in the day-to-day running of the club after he had 'retired'.

A succession of managers – Wilf McGuinness, Frank O'Farrell, Tommy Docherty, Dave Sexton and Ron Atkinson – would probably agree. His time as a director is remembered mainly for total incompetence on his part and that of the Old Trafford board. Like Ferguson later, he'd had problems finding a successor and for various reasons always made the wrong choice.

But that's enough. His death on 20 January 1991 ended the remarkable journey of a remarkable man and the only way I will remember him now is from a hot summer night at Wembley, the insufferable drama of extra time, the two symbolic goals from Charlton and the tears of the old man as he strode across the Wembley turf to embrace his players. It was the end of a long and painful journey and without him there would be no Manchester United today. No one, not even a foe, could argue with that. ●

> **It was always hard to dislike Busby. He had the mind of a successful politician: the right time to smile or frown, a gift for putting his fellow man at ease and always able to put names to faces. Even when quite young, he was seen as an avuncular figure, the father of football as some liked to call him.**